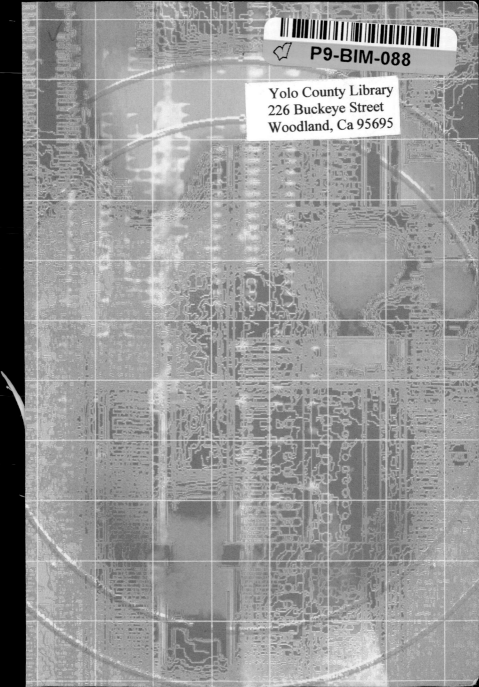

P9-BIM-088

Chaotic Century
Volume 14

Story and Art by
MICHIRO UEYAMA

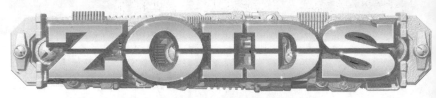

ZOIDS

Chaotic Century
Volume 14

Story and Art by **MICHIRO UEYAMA**

English Adaptation & Editing: William Flanagan
Translator: Kaori Kawakubo Inoue
Touch-up & Lettering: Dan Nakrosis
Cover Design/Benjamin Wright
Graphics & Design/Hidemi Sahara

Managing Editor: Annette Roman
VP of Sales & Marketing: Rick Bauer
Sr. V.P. of Editorial: Hyoe Narita
Publisher: Seiji Horibuchi

Printed in Canada.

Published by VIZ, LLC
P.O. Box 77010 • San Francisco, CA 94107

10 9 8 7 6 5 4 3 2 1
First printing, March 2003

WHY IS IT BACKWARDS?
ZOIDS was originally a Japanese comic (manga), and since
the Japanese read right-to-left, the comic you're reading is a
mirror image of the original drawings. So if you noticed that
the mark on Van's face is on the wrong side, that's why.

www.viz.com
• get your own vizmail.net email account
• register for the weekly email newsletter
• sign up for VIZ INternet

store.viz.com

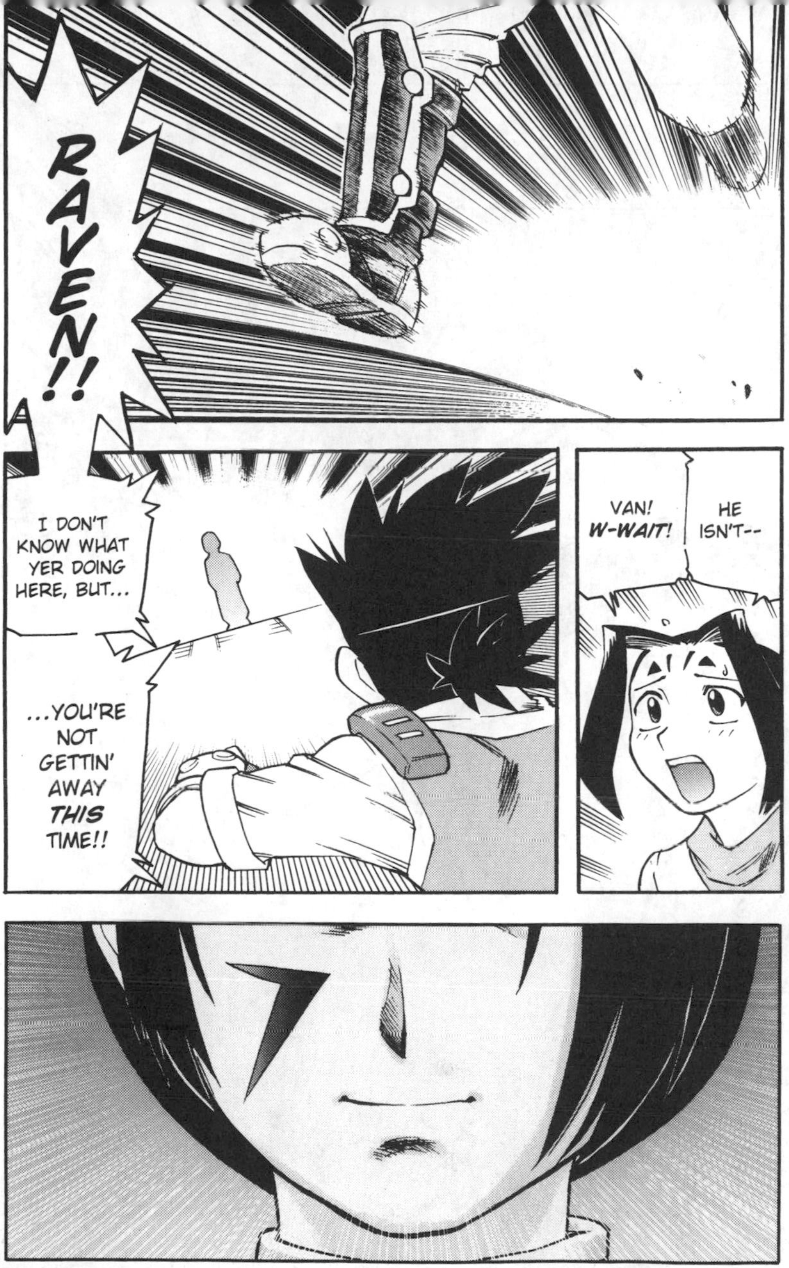

RAVEN!!
I DON'T KNOW WHAT YER DOING HERE, BUT...
...YOU'RE NOT GETTIN' AWAY THIS TIME!!
VAN! W-WAIT!
HE ISN'T--

The Eve of Zoids

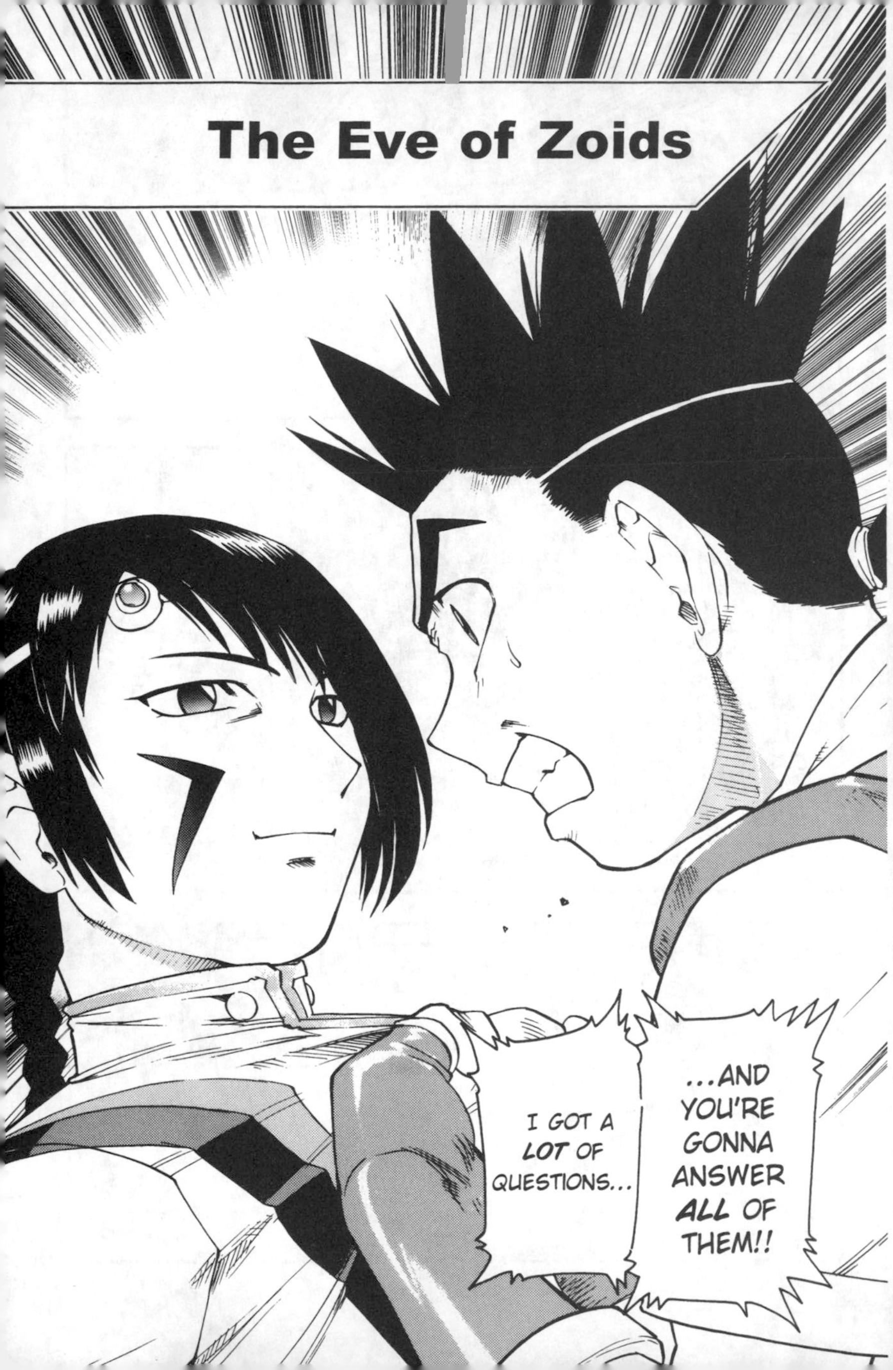
I GOT A *LOT* OF QUESTIONS...
...AND YOU'RE GONNA ANSWER *ALL* OF THEM!!

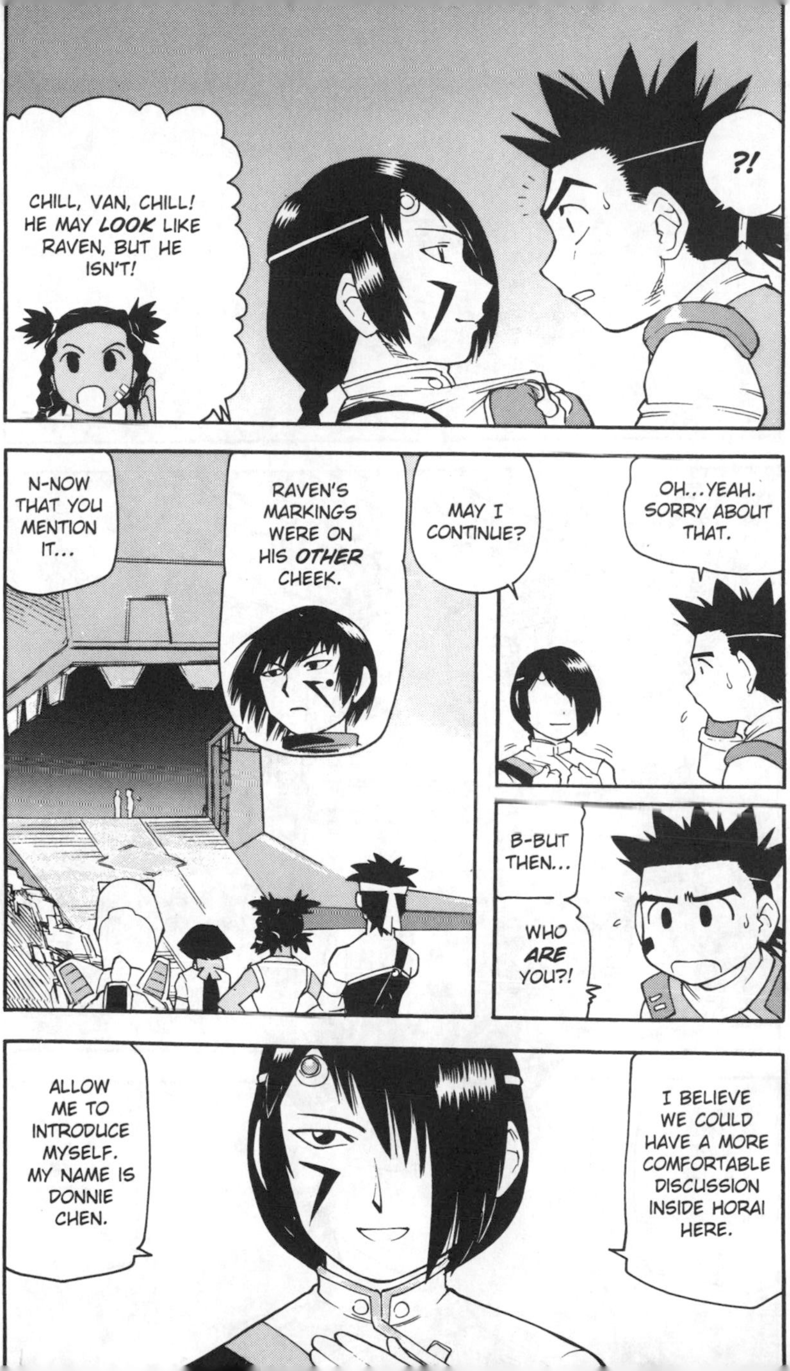
CHILL, VAN, CHILL! HE MAY LOOK LIKE RAVEN, BUT HE ISN'T!
?!
N-NOW THAT YOU MENTION IT...
RAVEN'S MARKINGS WERE ON HIS OTHER CHEEK.
MAY I CONTINUE?
OH...YEAH. SORRY ABOUT THAT.
B-BUT THEN...
WHO ARE YOU?!
ALLOW ME TO INTRODUCE MYSELF. MY NAME IS DONNIE CHEN.
I BELIEVE WE COULD HAVE A MORE COMFORTABLE DISCUSSION INSIDE HORAI HERE.

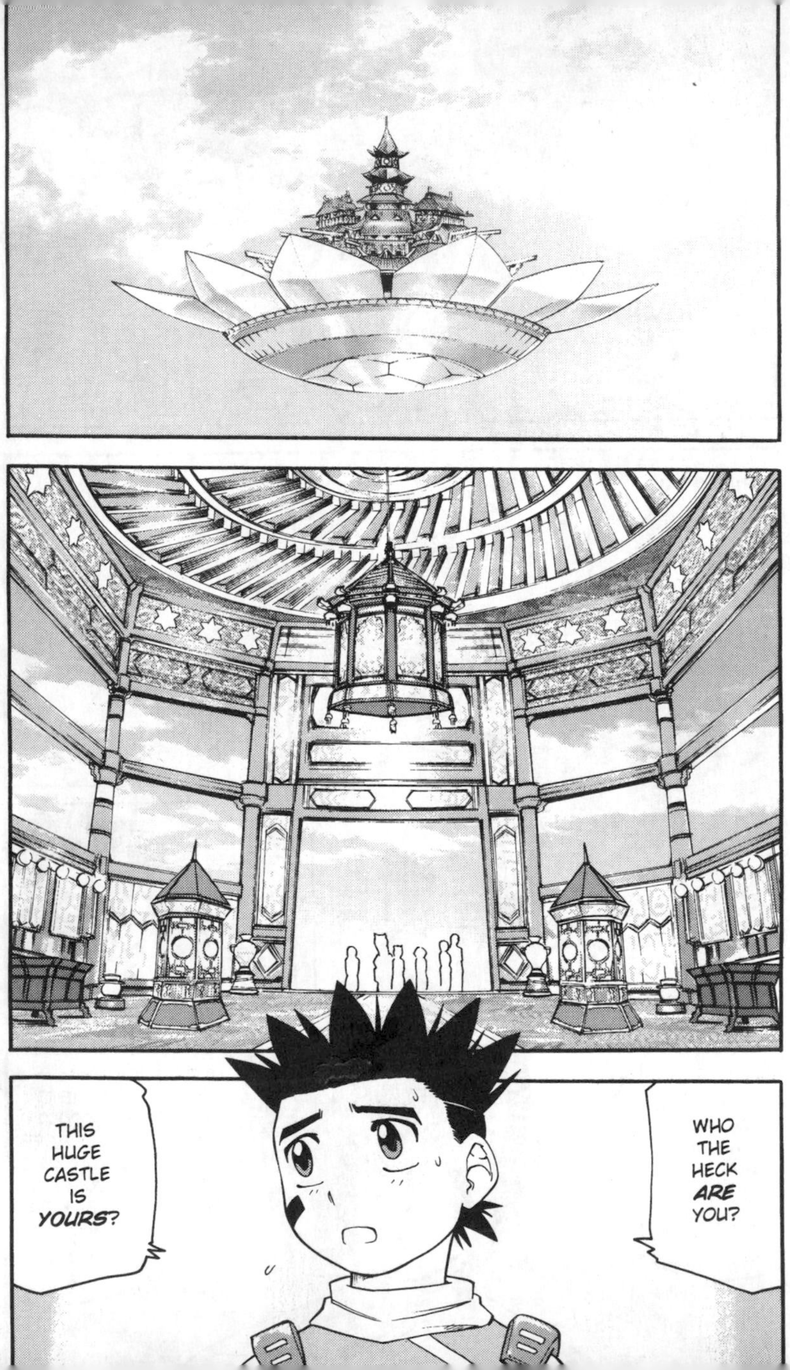
THIS HUGE CASTLE IS YOURS?
WHO THE HECK ARE YOU?

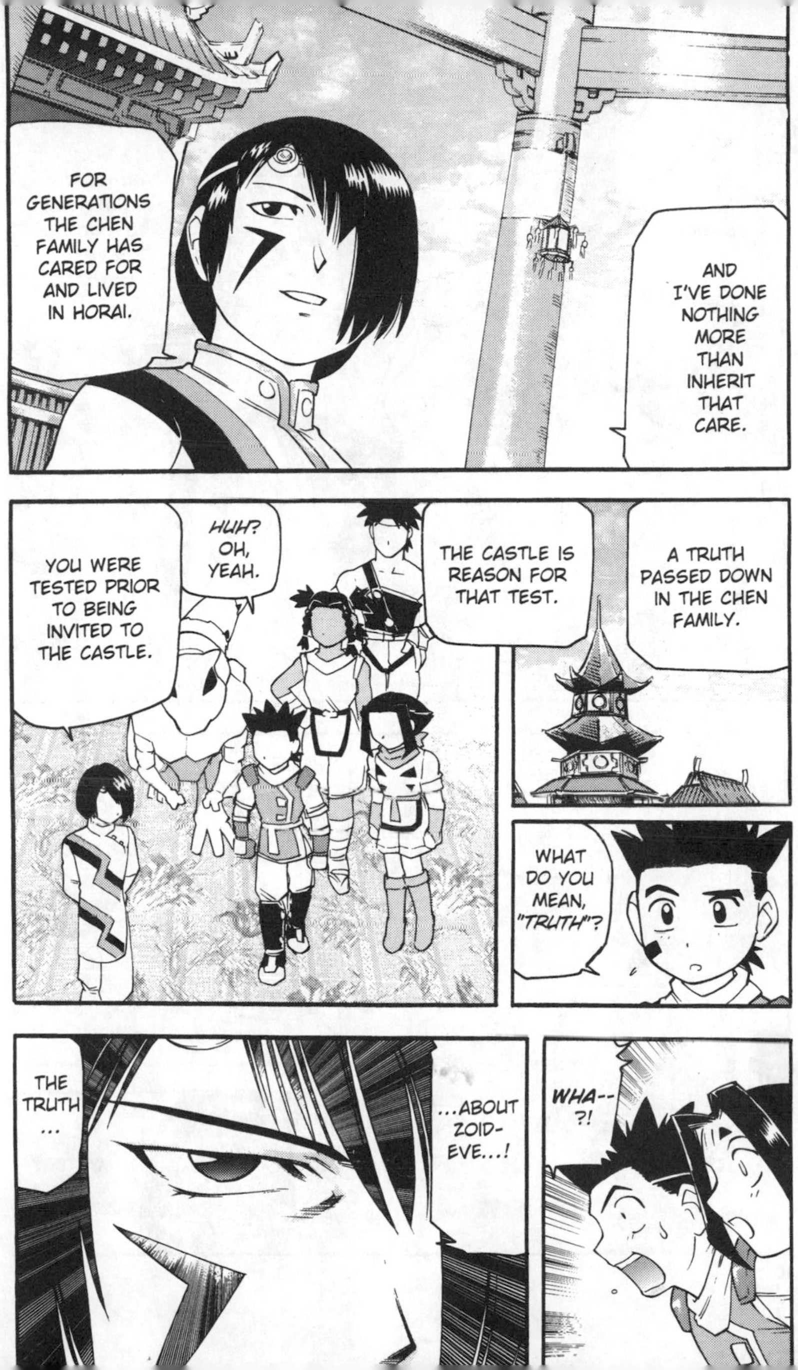
FOR GENERATIONS THE CHEN FAMILY HAS CARED FOR AND LIVED IN HORAI.
AND I'VE DONE NOTHING MORE THAN INHERIT THAT CARE.
YOU WERE TESTED PRIOR TO BEING INVITED TO THE CASTLE.
HUH? OH, YEAH.
THE CASTLE IS REASON FOR THAT TEST.
A TRUTH PASSED DOWN IN THE CHEN FAMILY.
WHAT DO YOU MEAN, "TRUTH"?
THE TRUTH ...
...ABOUT ZOID-EVE...!
WHA-- ?!

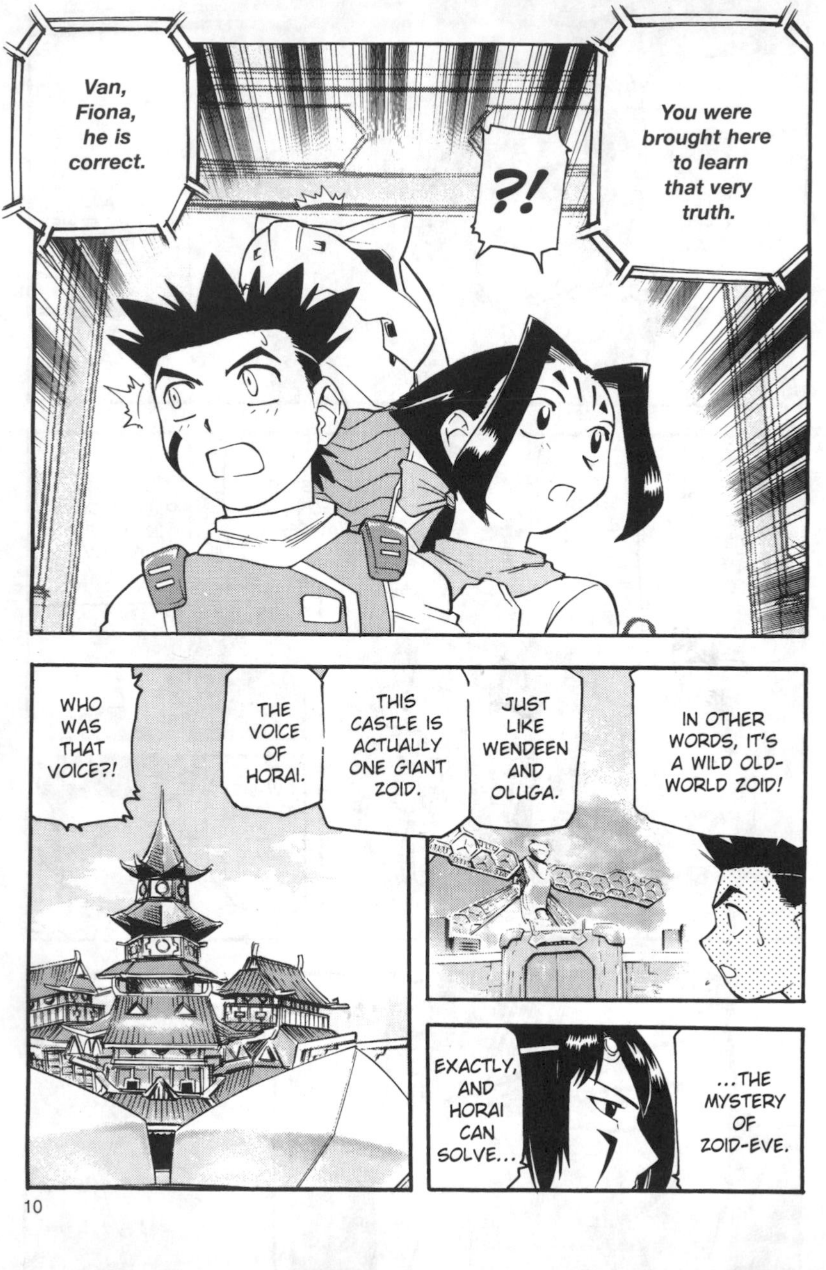
Van, Fiona, he is correct.
?!
You were brought here to learn that very truth.
WHO WAS THAT VOICE?!
THE VOICE OF HORAI.
THIS CASTLE IS ACTUALLY ONE GIANT ZOID.
JUST LIKE WENDEEN AND OLUGA.
IN OTHER WORDS, IT'S A WILD OLD-WORLD ZOID!
EXACTLY, AND HORAI CAN SOLVE...
...THE MYSTERY OF ZOID-EVE.

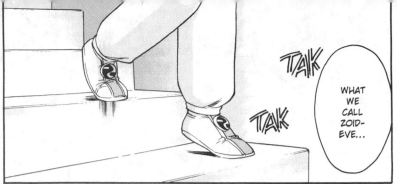

WHAT WE CALL ZOID-EVE...

...IS A MATTER THAT COULD TURN THE FATE OF THE ENTIRE PLANET!

THEREFORE, HORAI WILL ONLY REVEAL THIS KNOWLEDGE TO A SELECT FEW.

SO I CAN ASK--

RATHER, I CAN ACTUALLY *TALK* TO HORAI?

ZOIDS LIKE WENDEEN EXPRESS THOUGHTS THROUGH AN EMOTIONAL LINK.

HOWEVER, ONE CAN ACTUALLY CONVERSE WITH HORAI WHEN ONE IS IN THE CORE.

AND THIS...

KANK KAAAA

...IS THAT ROOM!

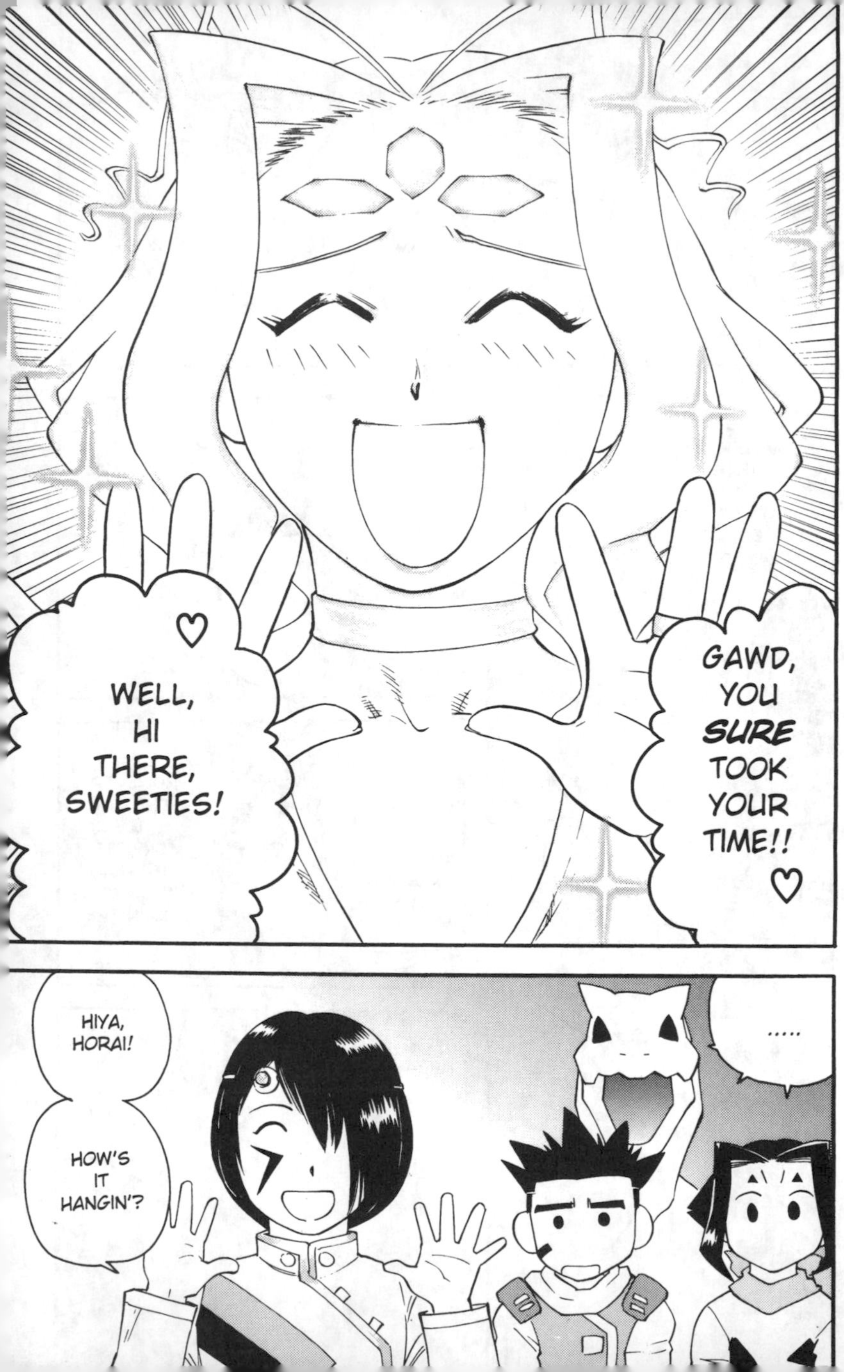
WELL, HI THERE, SWEETIES! ♡
GAWD, YOU *SURE* TOOK YOUR TIME!! ♡
HIYA, HORAI!
HOW'S IT HANGIN'?
.....

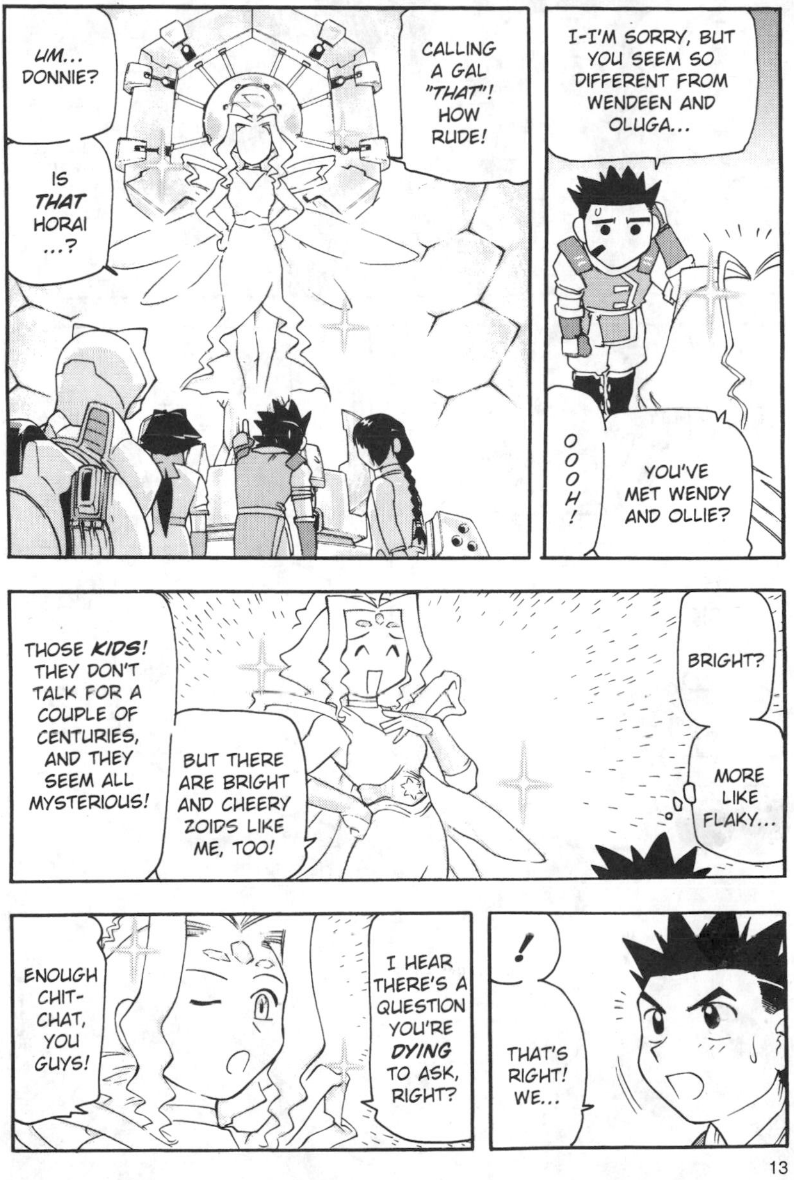
UM... DONNIE?
IS *THAT* HORAI ...?
CALLING A GAL "*THAT*"! HOW RUDE!
I-I'M SORRY, BUT YOU SEEM SO DIFFERENT FROM WENDEEN AND OLUGA...
OOOH!
YOU'VE MET WENDY AND OLLIE?
THOSE *KIDS*! THEY DON'T TALK FOR A COUPLE OF CENTURIES, AND THEY SEEM ALL MYSTERIOUS!
BUT THERE ARE BRIGHT AND CHEERY ZOIDS LIKE ME, TOO!
BRIGHT?
MORE LIKE FLAKY...
ENOUGH CHIT-CHAT, YOU GUYS!
I HEAR THERE'S A QUESTION YOU'RE *DYING* TO ASK, RIGHT?
!
THAT'S RIGHT! WE...

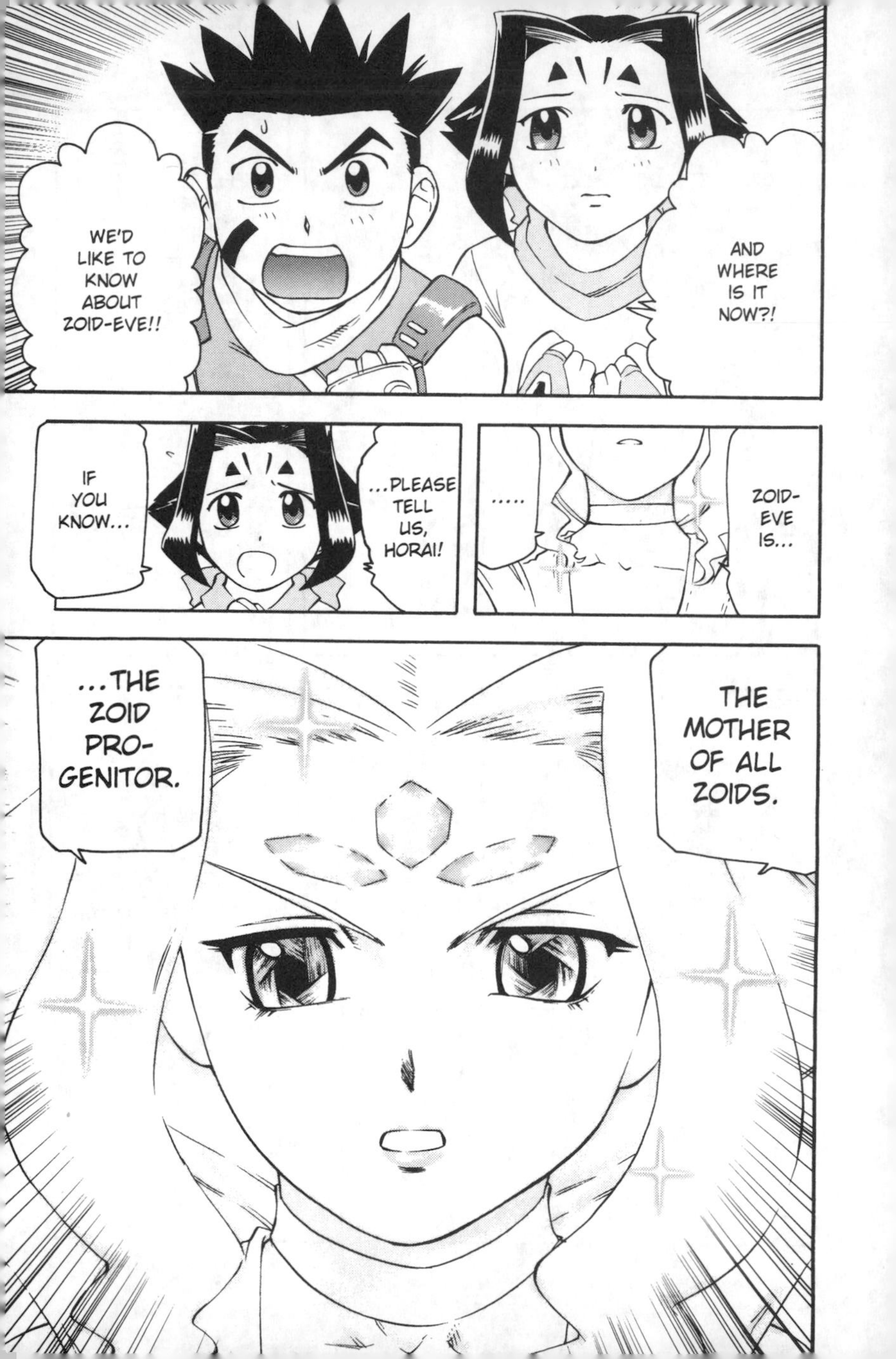
WE'D LIKE TO KNOW ABOUT ZOID-EVE!!
AND WHERE IS IT NOW?!
IF YOU KNOW...
...PLEASE TELL US, HORAI!
.....
ZOID-EVE IS...
...THE ZOID PRO-GENITOR.
THE MOTHER OF ALL ZOIDS.

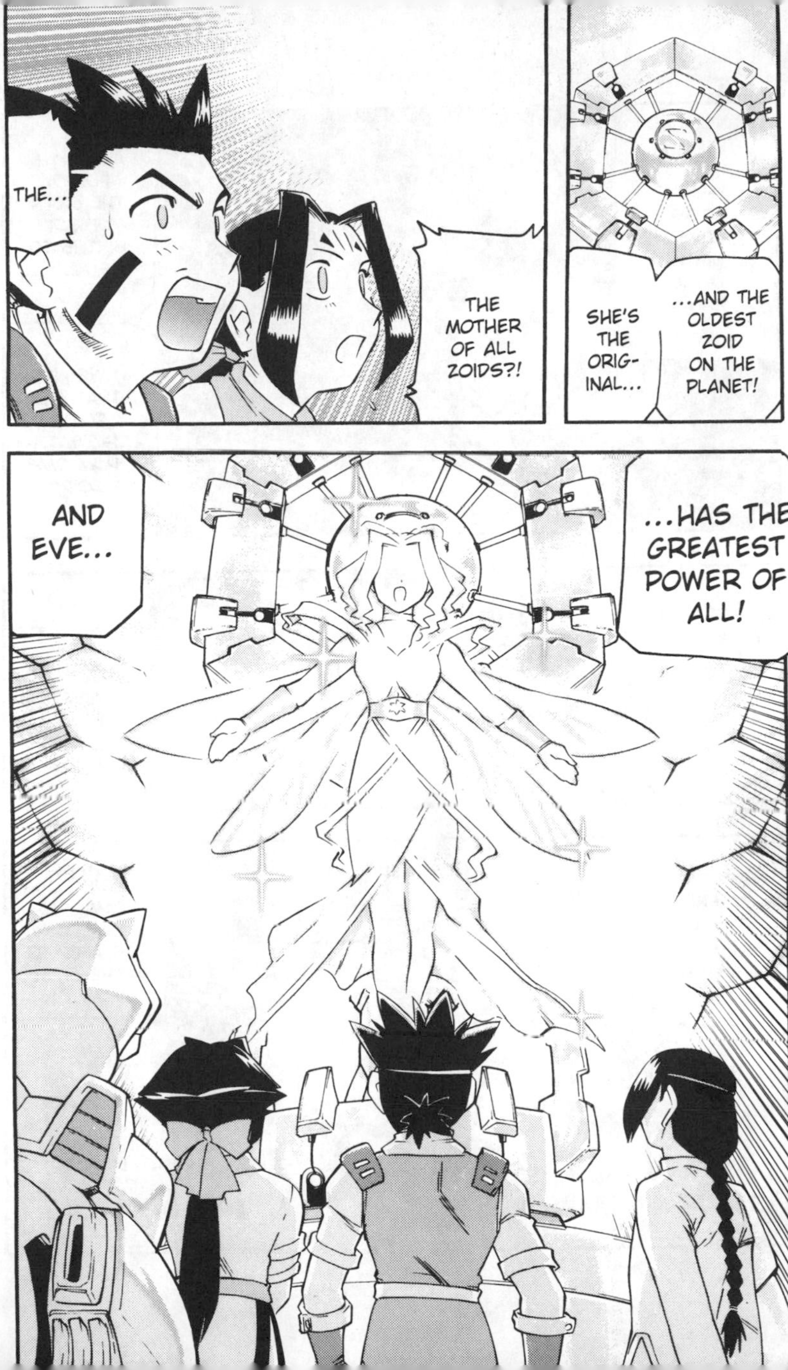
THE...
THE MOTHER OF ALL ZOIDS?!
SHE'S THE ORIG-INAL...
...AND THE OLDEST ZOID ON THE PLANET!
AND EVE...
...HAS THE GREATEST POWER OF ALL!

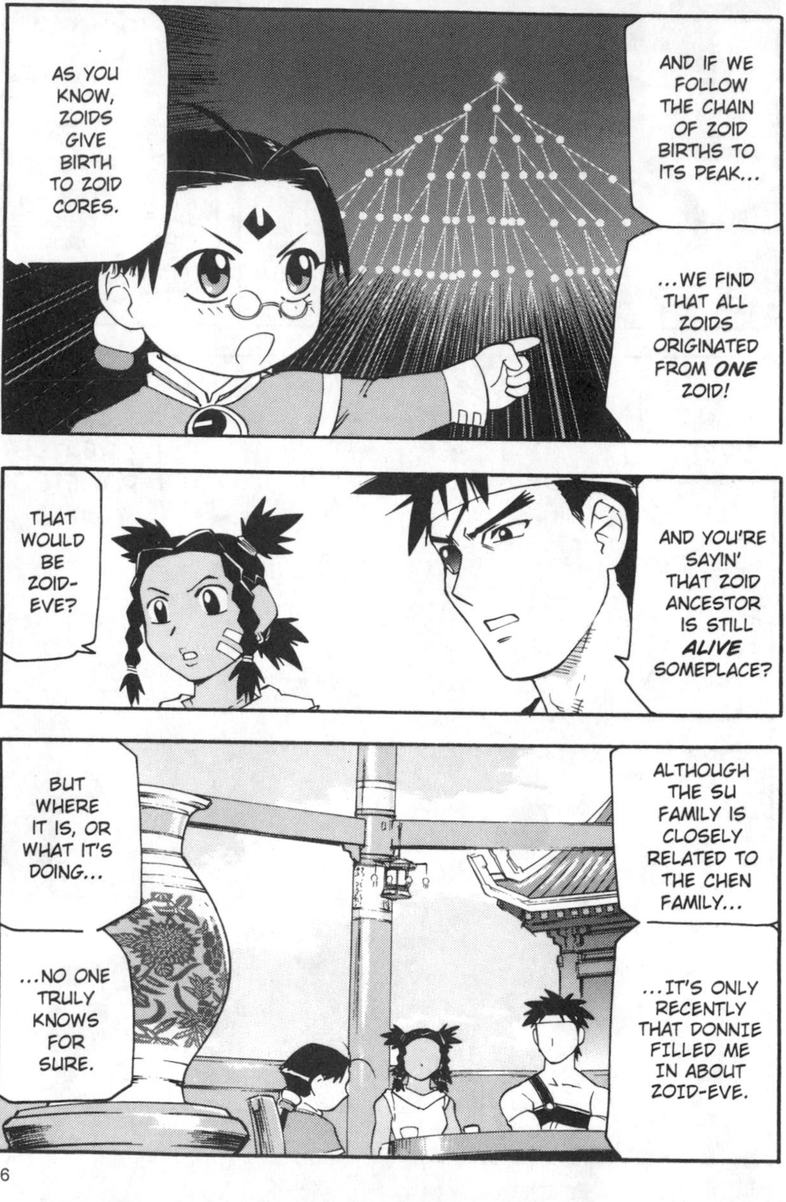
AS YOU KNOW, ZOIDS GIVE BIRTH TO ZOID CORES.
AND IF WE FOLLOW THE CHAIN OF ZOID BIRTHS TO ITS PEAK...
...WE FIND THAT ALL ZOIDS ORIGINATED FROM *ONE* ZOID!
THAT WOULD BE ZOID-EVE?
AND YOU'RE SAYIN' THAT ZOID ANCESTOR IS STILL *ALIVE* SOMEPLACE?
BUT WHERE IT IS, OR WHAT IT'S DOING...
...NO ONE TRULY KNOWS FOR SURE.
ALTHOUGH THE SU FAMILY IS CLOSELY RELATED TO THE CHEN FAMILY...
...IT'S ONLY RECENTLY THAT DONNIE FILLED ME IN ABOUT ZOID-EVE.

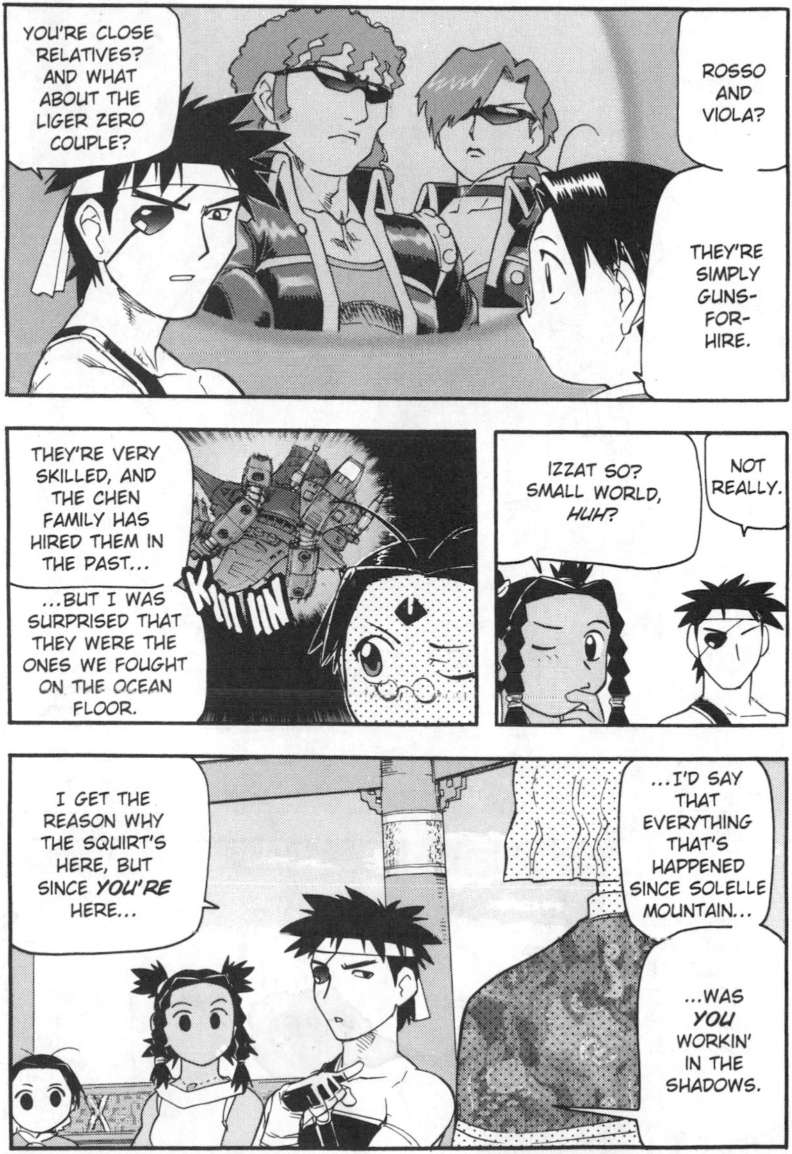
YOU'RE CLOSE RELATIVES? AND WHAT ABOUT THE LIGER ZERO COUPLE?
ROSSO AND VIOLA?
THEY'RE SIMPLY GUNS-FOR-HIRE.
THEY'RE VERY SKILLED, AND THE CHEN FAMILY HAS HIRED THEM IN THE PAST...
...BUT I WAS SURPRISED THAT THEY WERE THE ONES WE FOUGHT ON THE OCEAN FLOOR.
KIIIIIN
IZZAT SO? SMALL WORLD, *HUH?*
NOT REALLY.
I GET THE REASON WHY THE SQUIRT'S HERE, BUT SINCE *YOU'RE* HERE...
...I'D SAY THAT EVERYTHING THAT'S HAPPENED SINCE SOLELLE MOUNTAIN...
...WAS *YOU* WORKIN' IN THE SHADOWS.

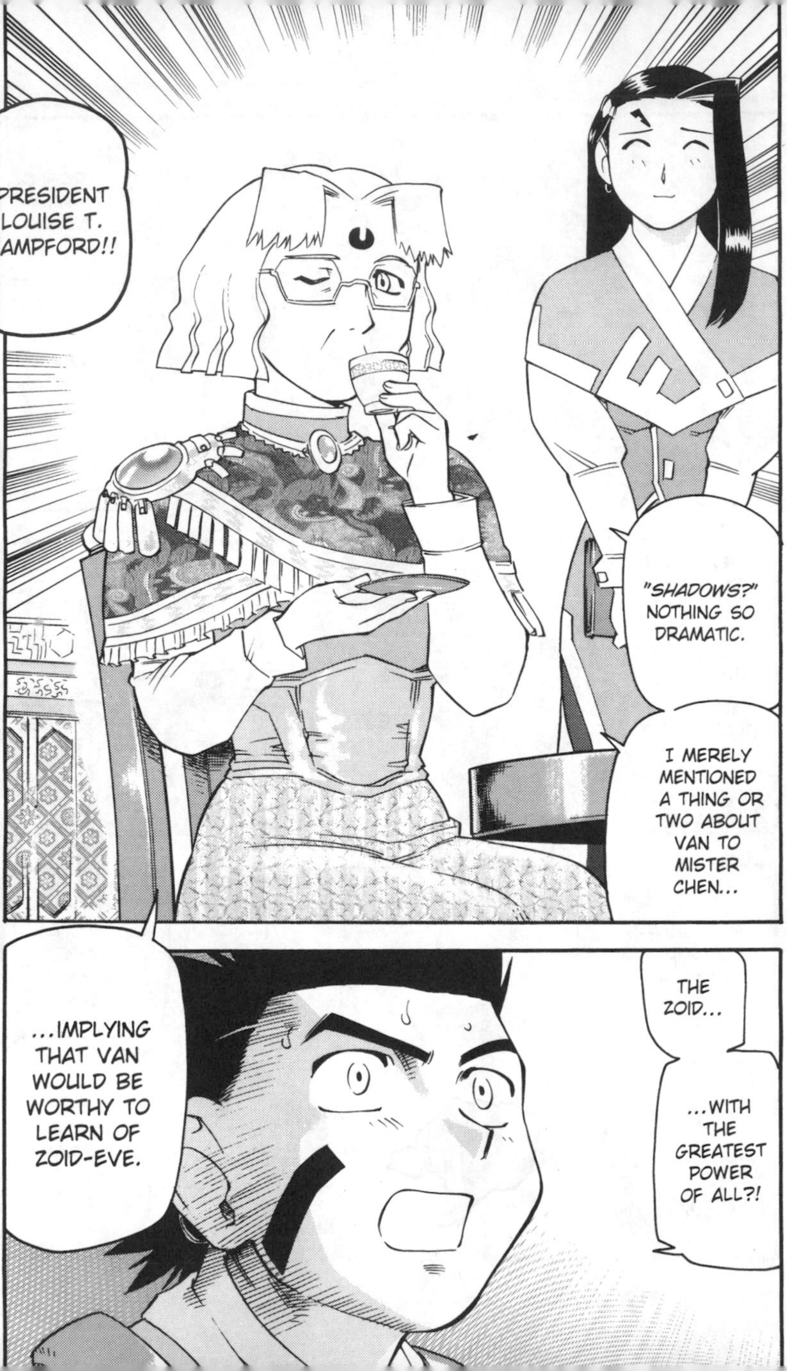
PRESIDENT LOUISE T. CAMPFORD!!
"SHADOWS?" NOTHING SO DRAMATIC.
I MERELY MENTIONED A THING OR TWO ABOUT VAN TO MISTER CHEN...
...IMPLYING THAT VAN WOULD BE WORTHY TO LEARN OF ZOID-EVE.
THE ZOID...
...WITH THE GREATEST POWER OF ALL?!

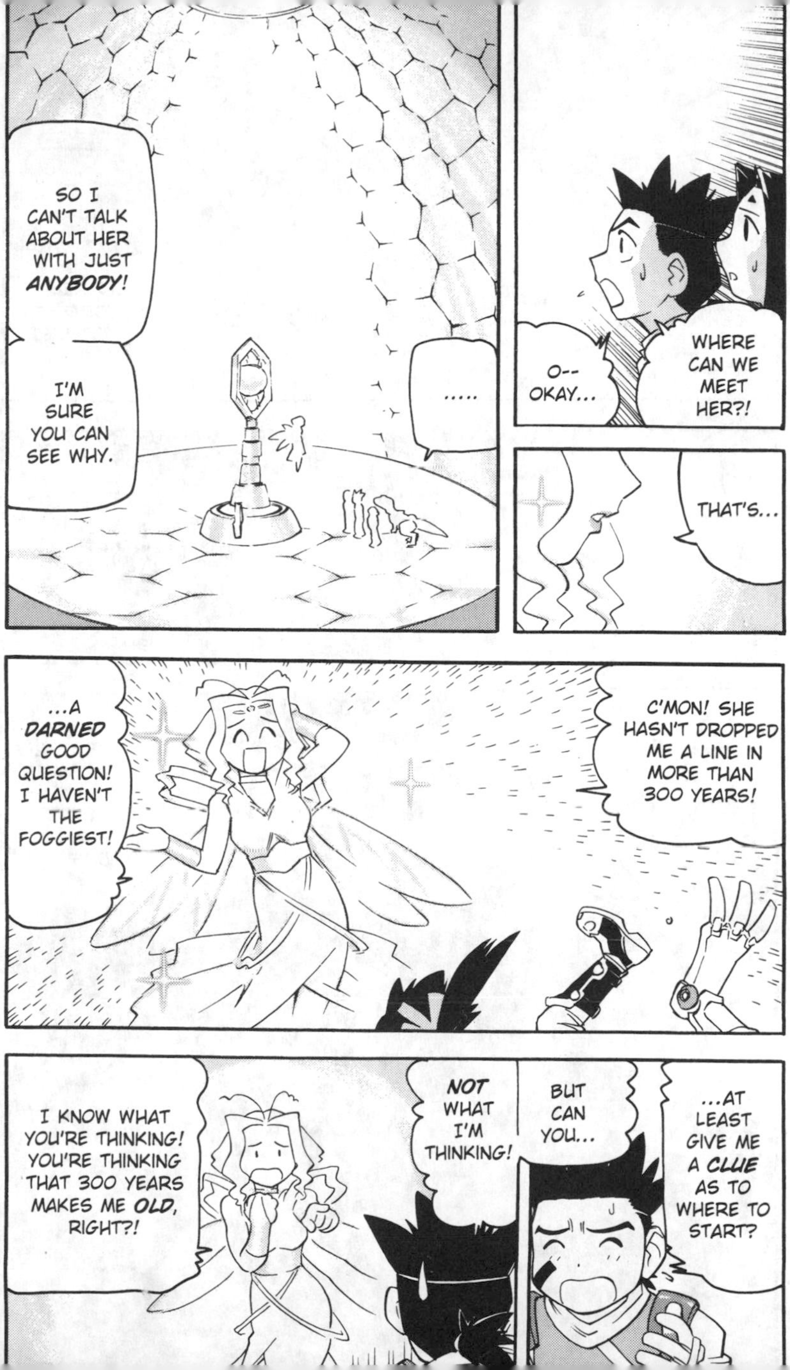
SO I CAN'T TALK ABOUT HER WITH JUST ANYBODY!
I'M SURE YOU CAN SEE WHY.
.....
O-- OKAY...
WHERE CAN WE MEET HER?!
THAT'S...
...A DARNED GOOD QUESTION! I HAVEN'T THE FOGGIEST!
C'MON! SHE HASN'T DROPPED ME A LINE IN MORE THAN 300 YEARS!
I KNOW WHAT YOU'RE THINKING! YOU'RE THINKING THAT 300 YEARS MAKES ME OLD, RIGHT?!
NOT WHAT I'M THINKING!
BUT CAN YOU...
...AT LEAST GIVE ME A CLUE AS TO WHERE TO START?

THERE ARE CLUES TO BE FOUND.

THERE'S ONE WHICH YOU'VE ALREADY COME INTO CONTACT WITH...

?!

ALREADY IN CONTACT?!

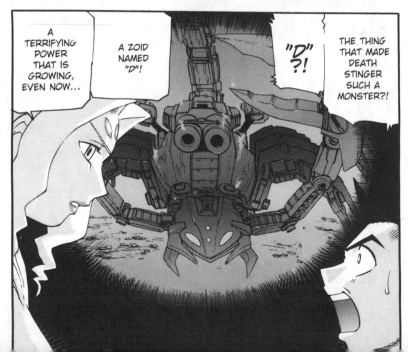

A TERRIFYING POWER THAT IS GROWING, EVEN NOW...

A ZOID NAMED "D"!

"D"?!

THE THING THAT MADE DEATH STINGER SUCH A MONSTER?!

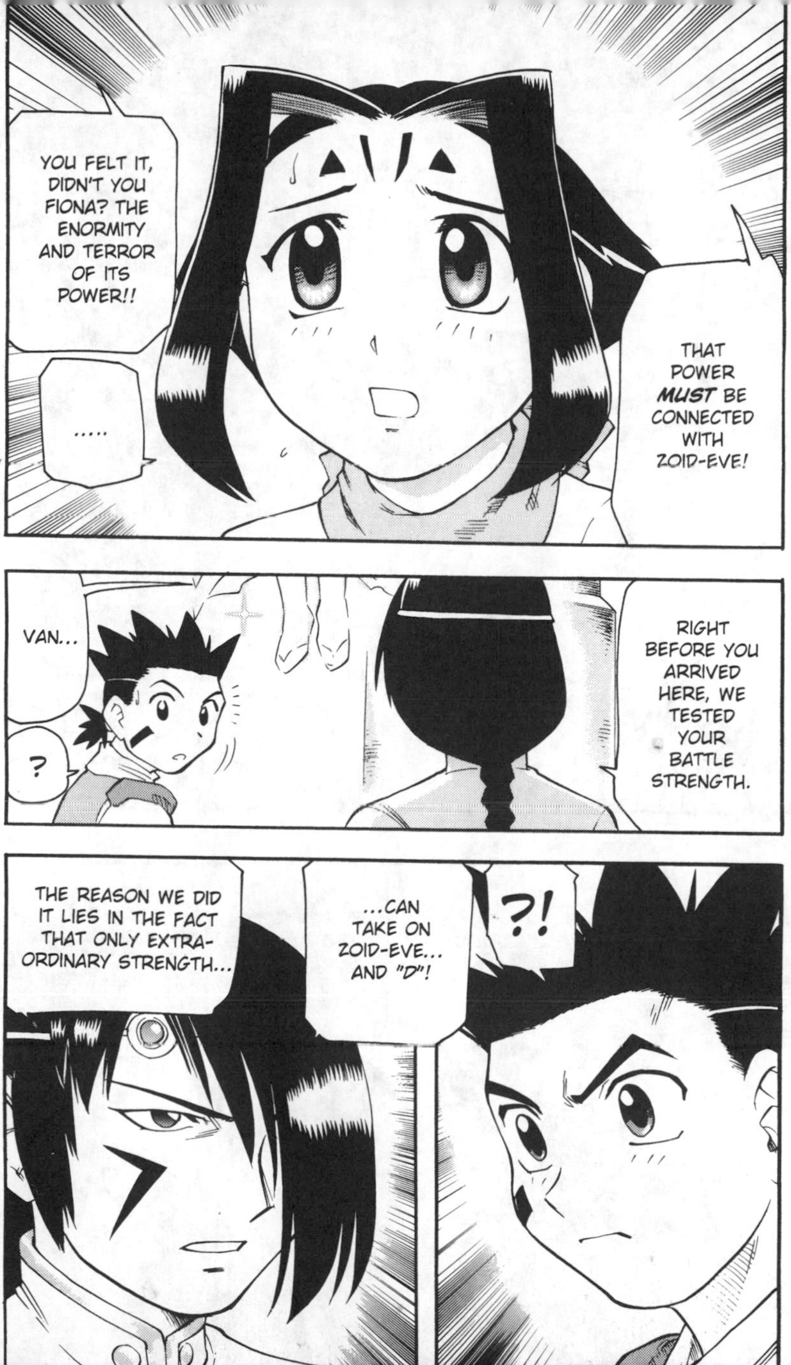
YOU FELT IT, DIDN'T YOU FIONA? THE ENORMITY AND TERROR OF ITS POWER!!
.....
THAT POWER MUST BE CONNECTED WITH ZOID-EVE!
VAN...
?
RIGHT BEFORE YOU ARRIVED HERE, WE TESTED YOUR BATTLE STRENGTH.
THE REASON WE DID IT LIES IN THE FACT THAT ONLY EXTRA-ORDINARY STRENGTH...
...CAN TAKE ON ZOID-EVE... AND "D"!
?!

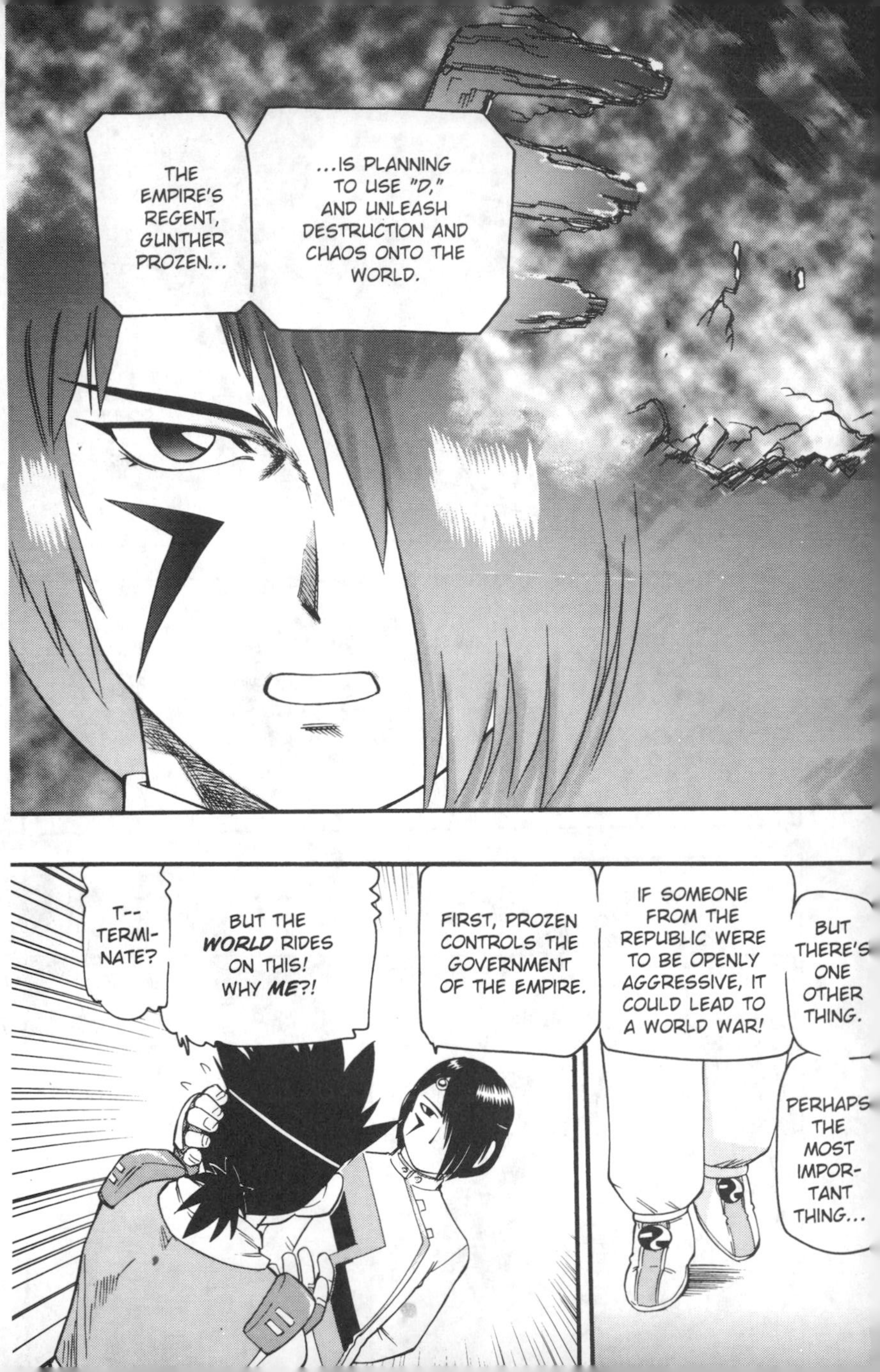
THE EMPIRE'S REGENT, GUNTHER PROZEN...
...IS PLANNING TO USE "D," AND UNLEASH DESTRUCTION AND CHAOS ONTO THE WORLD.
T-- TERMI-NATE?
BUT THE WORLD RIDES ON THIS! WHY ME?!
FIRST, PROZEN CONTROLS THE GOVERNMENT OF THE EMPIRE.
IF SOMEONE FROM THE REPUBLIC WERE TO BE OPENLY AGGRESSIVE, IT COULD LEAD TO A WORLD WAR!
BUT THERE'S ONE OTHER THING.
PERHAPS THE MOST IMPOR-TANT THING...

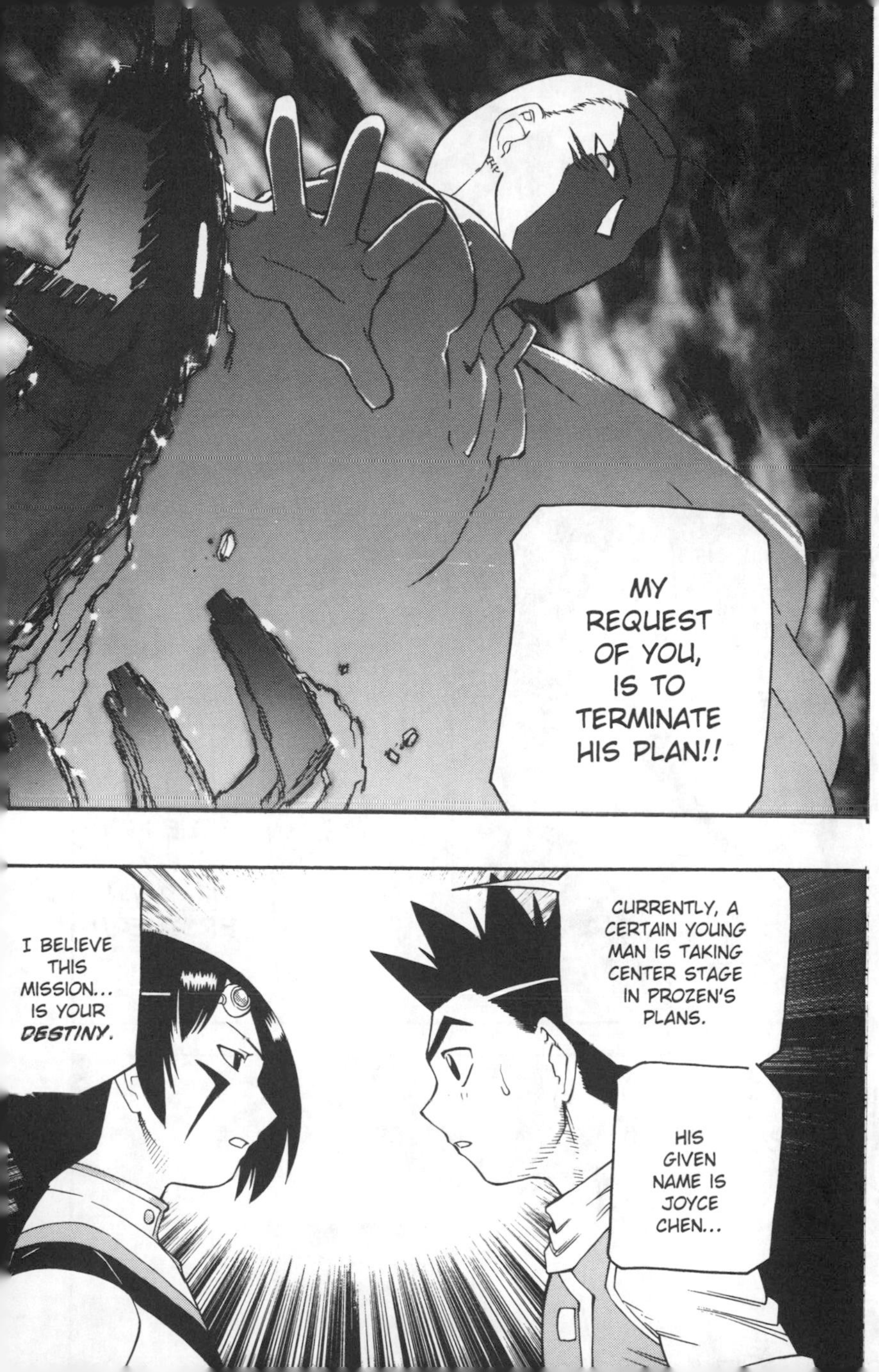
MY REQUEST OF YOU, IS TO TERMINATE HIS PLAN!!
I BELIEVE THIS MISSION... IS YOUR DESTINY.
CURRENTLY, A CERTAIN YOUNG MAN IS TAKING CENTER STAGE IN PROZEN'S PLANS.
HIS GIVEN NAME IS JOYCE CHEN...

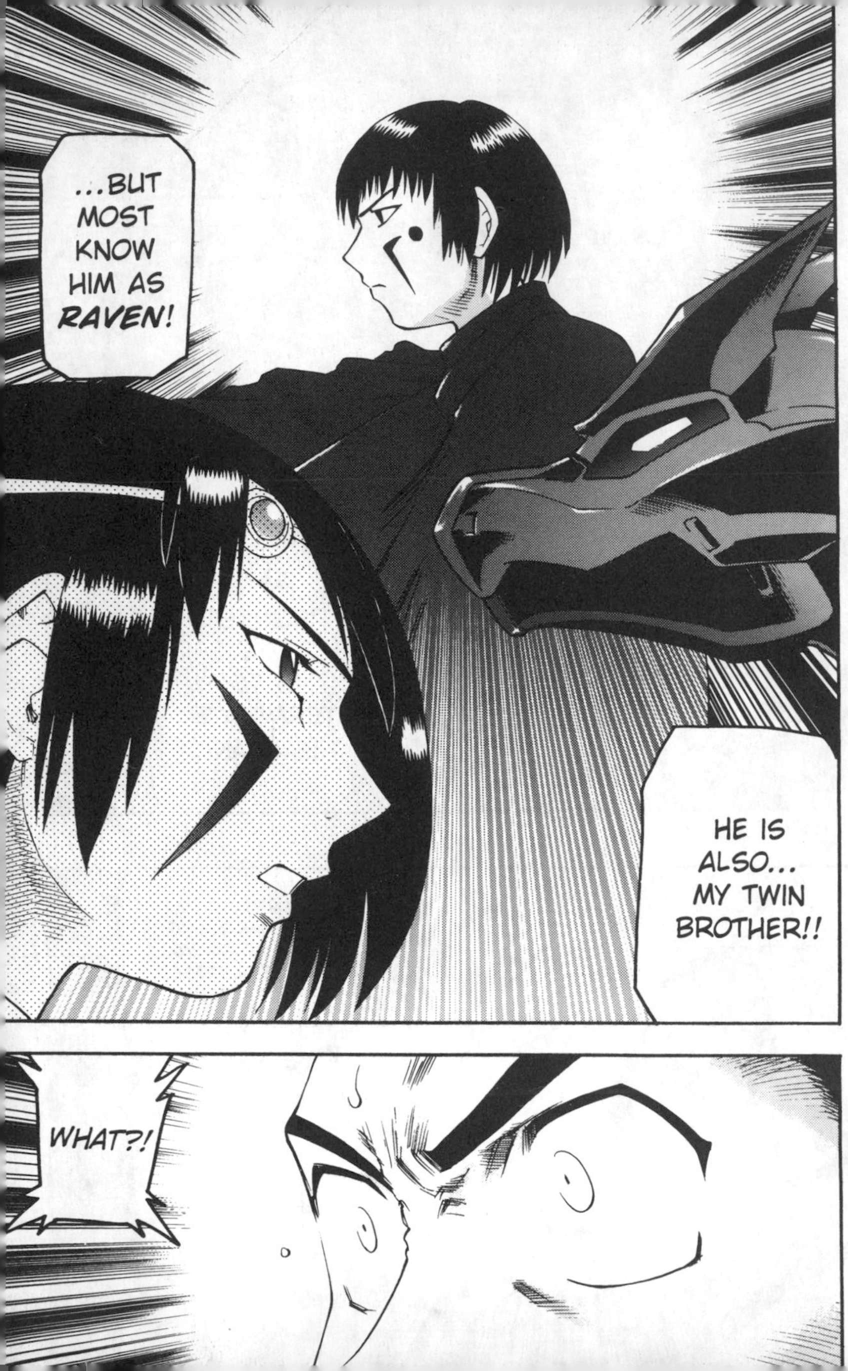
...BUT MOST KNOW HIM AS RAVEN!
HE IS ALSO... MY TWIN BROTHER!!
WHAT?!

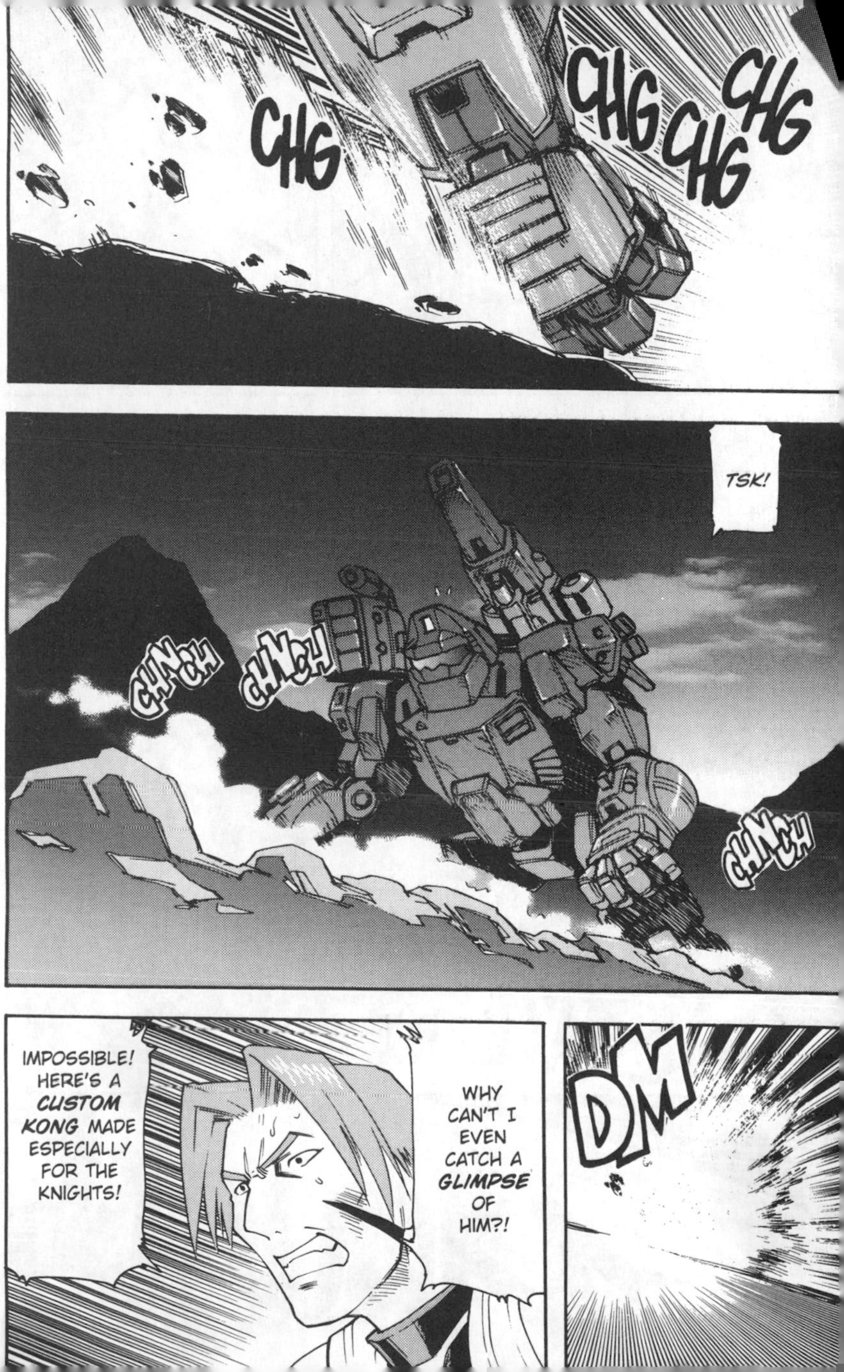
CHG
CHG CHG CHG
CHNCH
CHNCH
CHNCH
TSK!
IMPOSSIBLE! HERE'S A CUSTOM KONG MADE ESPECIALLY FOR THE KNIGHTS!
WHY CAN'T I EVEN CATCH A GLIMPSE OF HIM?!
DM

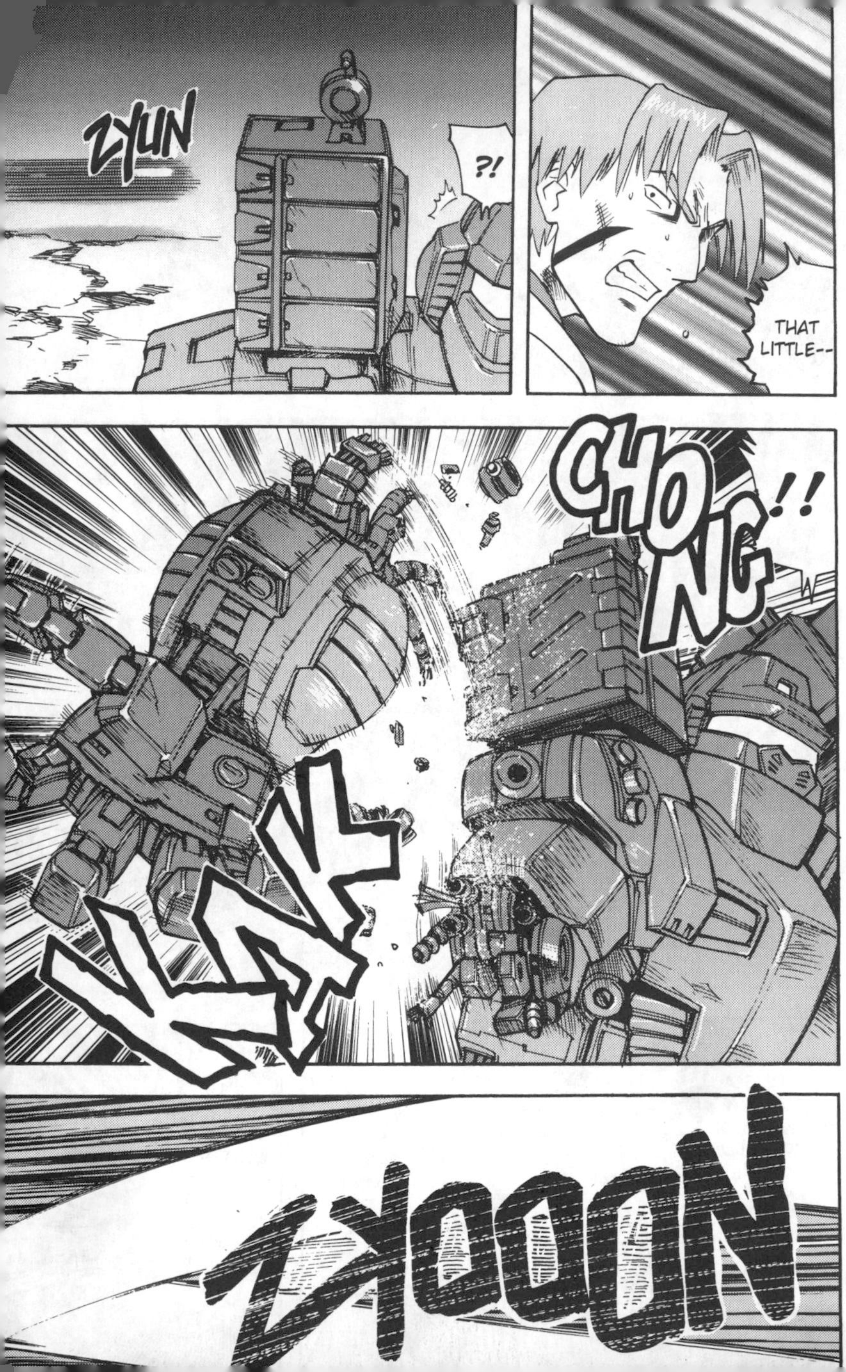
ZYUN
?!
THAT LITTLE--
CHONG!!
ZYOOON

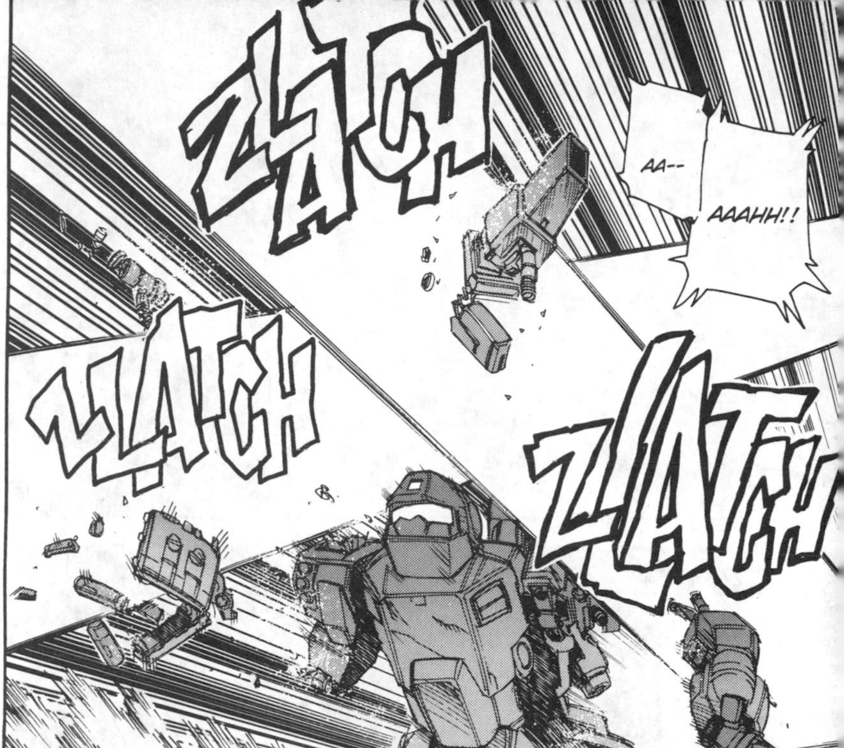
AA--
AAAHH!!
ZLACH
ZLACH
ZLATCH

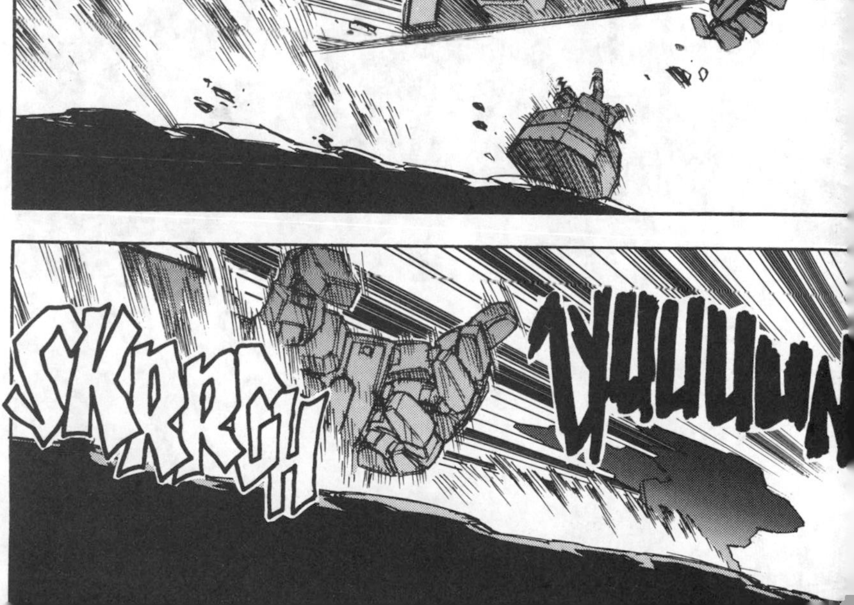
SKRRCH

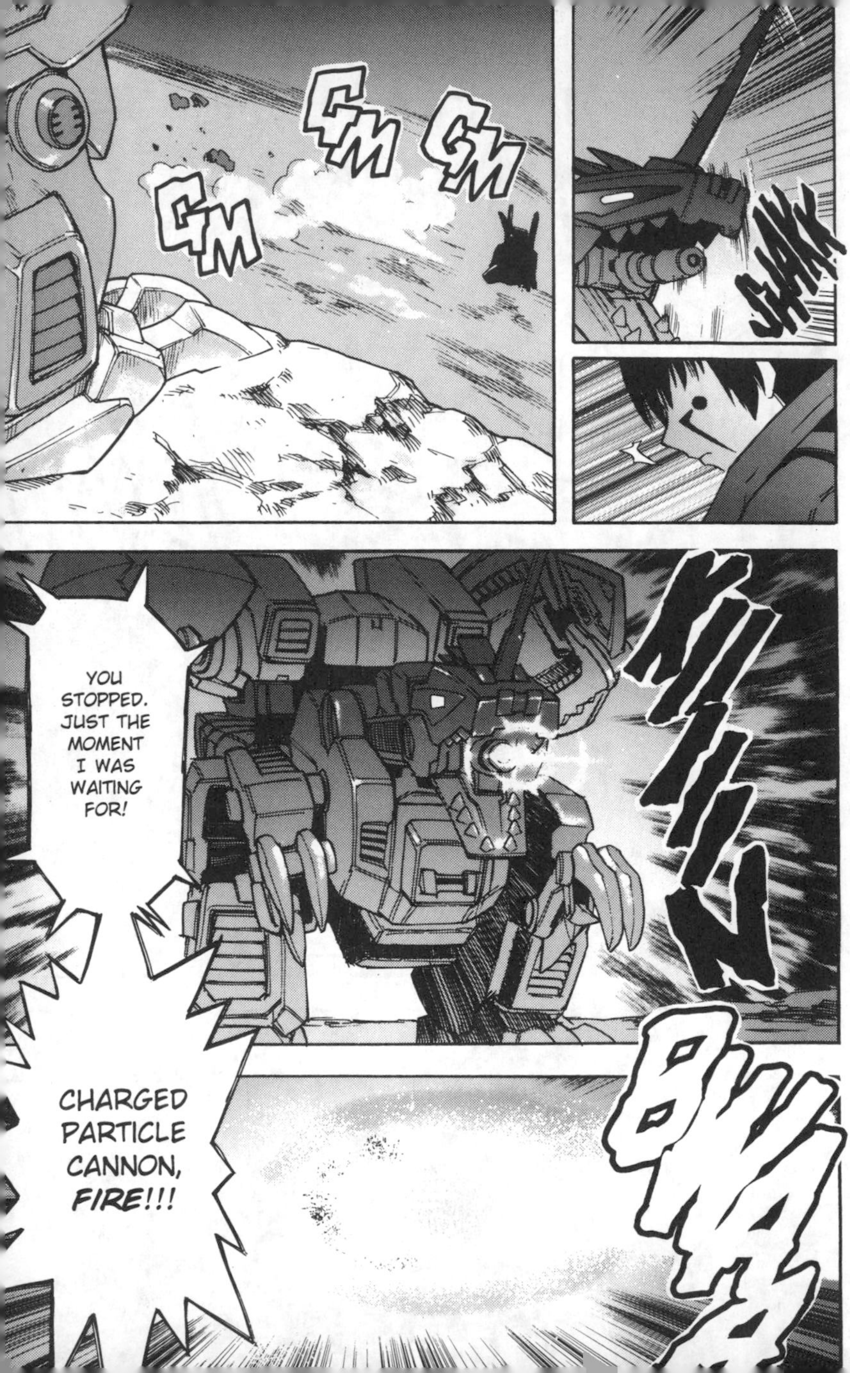
GM
GM GM
GAKK
YOU STOPPED. JUST THE MOMENT I WAS WAITING FOR!
KIIIN
CHARGED PARTICLE CANNON, *FIRE*!!!
BWA

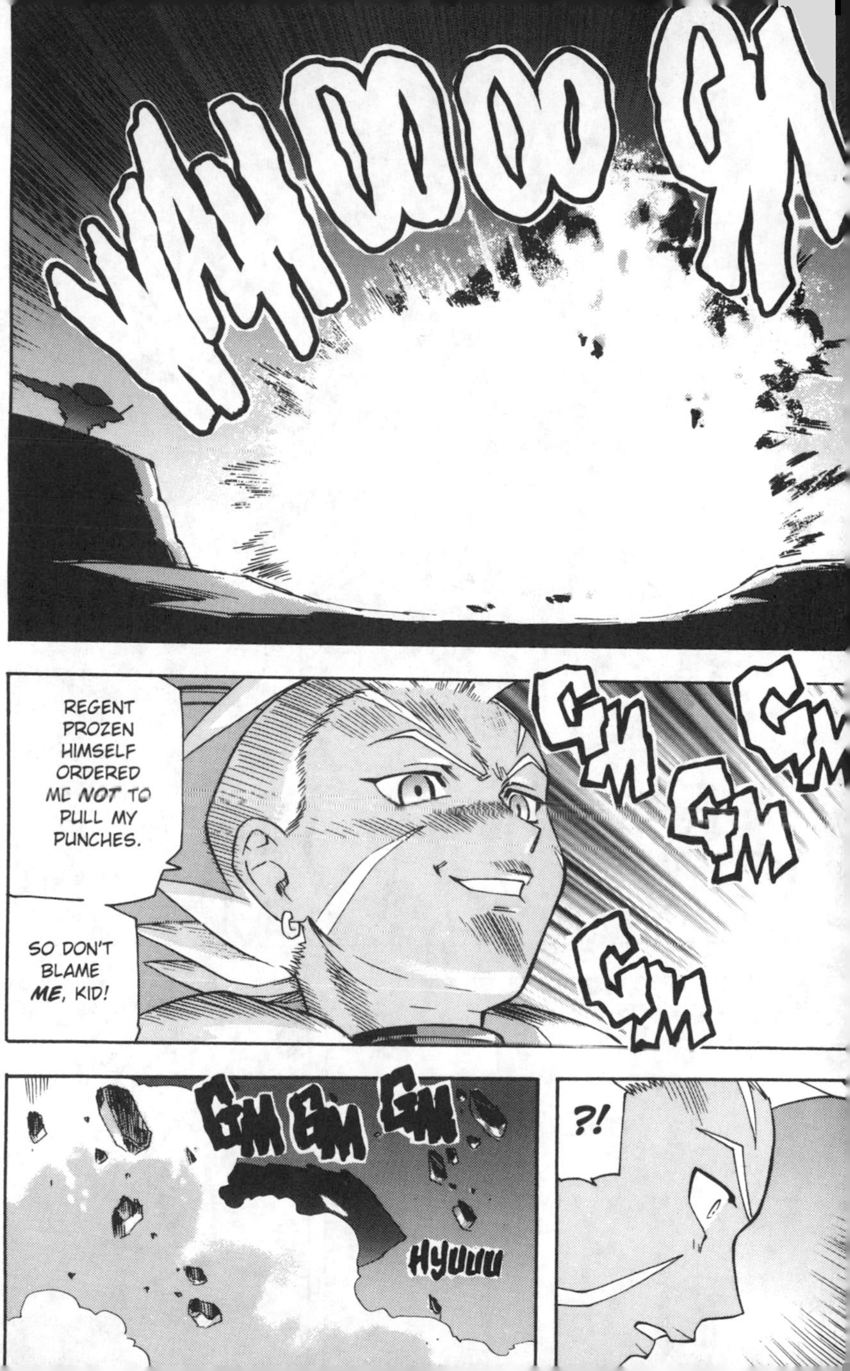
WAHOOO
REGENT PROZEN HIMSELF ORDERED ME *NOT* TO PULL MY PUNCHES.
SO DON'T BLAME *ME*, KID!
GM GM GM GM
GM
GM GM GM
HYUUU
?!

M DM DM DM DM

I--
IT'S... ...UNDAM-
AGED?!

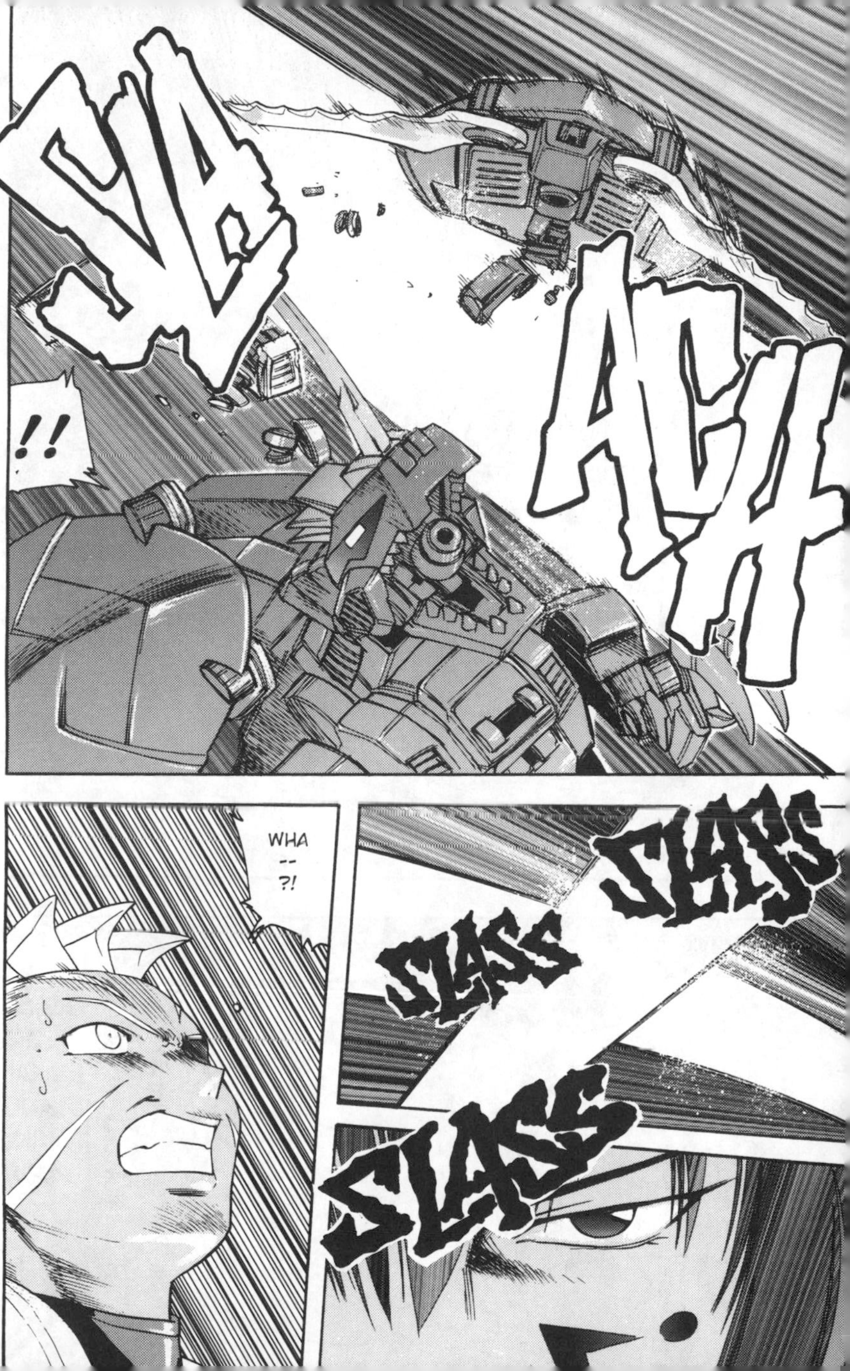
ZA
ACH
!!
WHA
--
?!
SLASS
SLASS
SLASS

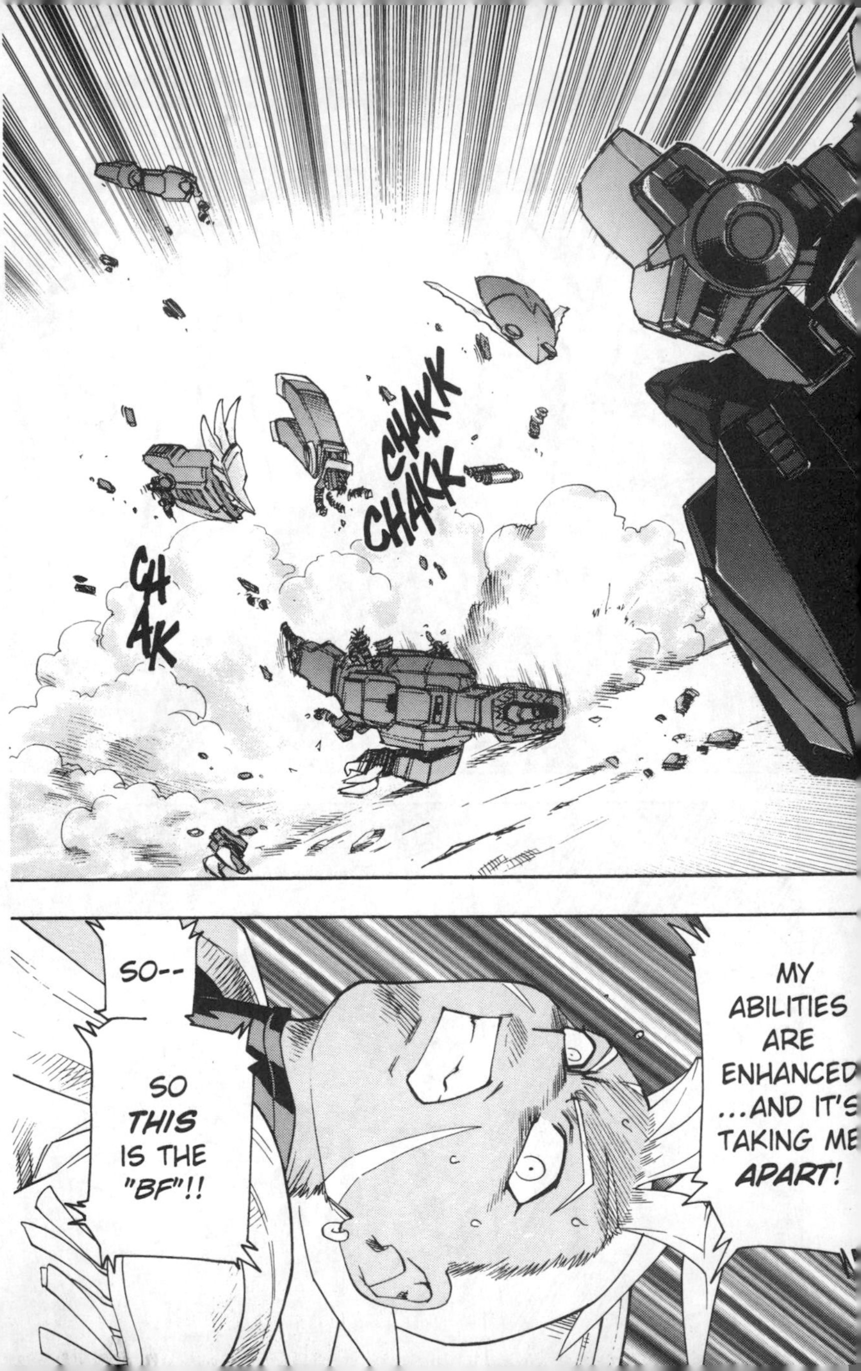
CHAK
CHAKK CHAKK
SO--
SO *THIS* IS THE "*BF*"!!
MY ABILITIES ARE ENHANCED ...AND IT'S TAKING ME *APART*!

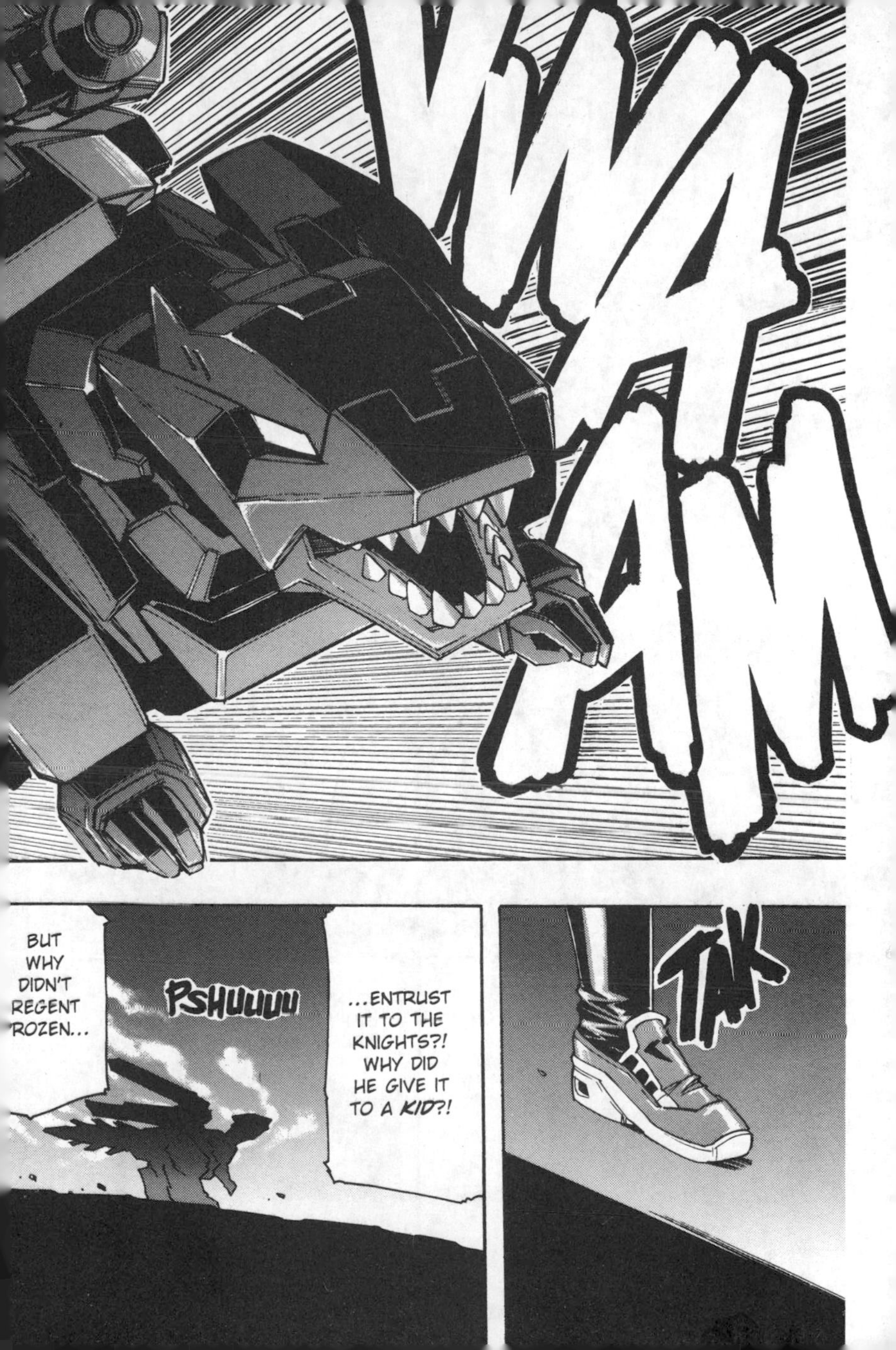
WHAM
BUT WHY DIDN'T REGENT ROZEN...
PSHUUUU
...ENTRUST IT TO THE KNIGHTS?! WHY DID HE GIVE IT TO A *KID*?!
TAK

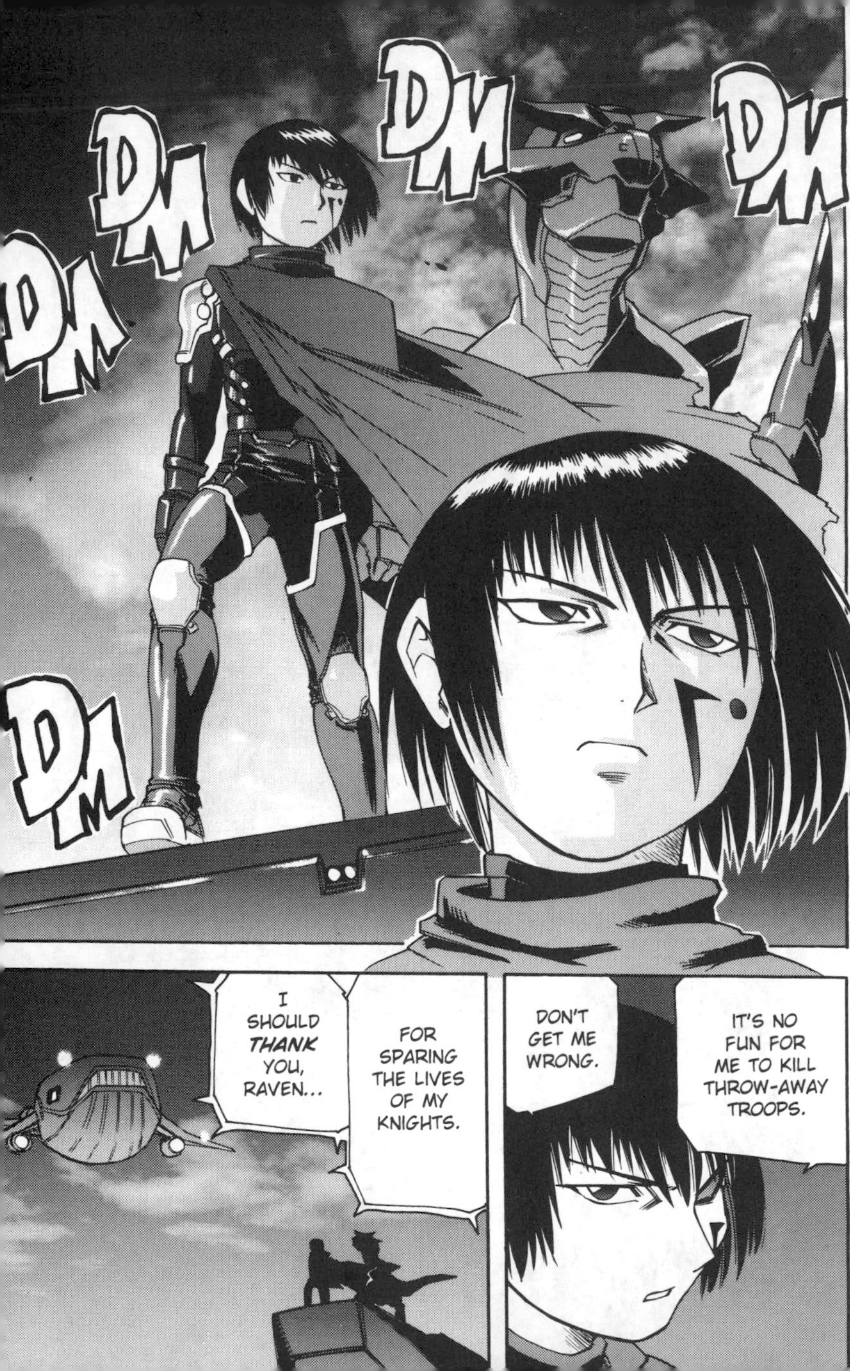
DM
DM
DM
DM
DM
I SHOULD *THANK* YOU, RAVEN...
FOR SPARING THE LIVES OF MY KNIGHTS.
DON'T GET ME WRONG.
IT'S NO FUN FOR ME TO KILL THROW-AWAY TROOPS.

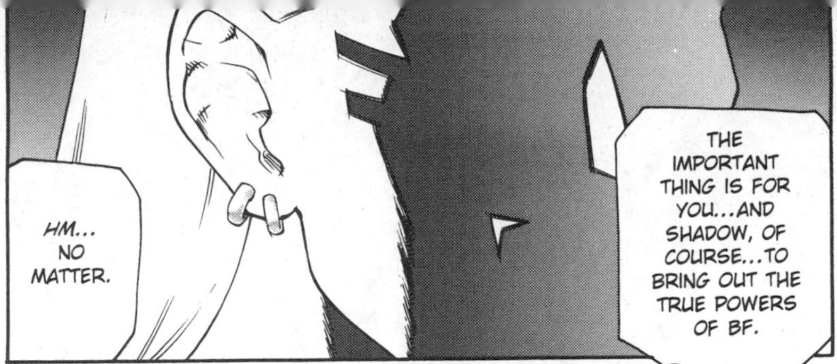
HM... NO MATTER.
THE IMPORTANT THING IS FOR YOU...AND SHADOW, OF COURSE...TO BRING OUT THE TRUE POWERS OF BF.

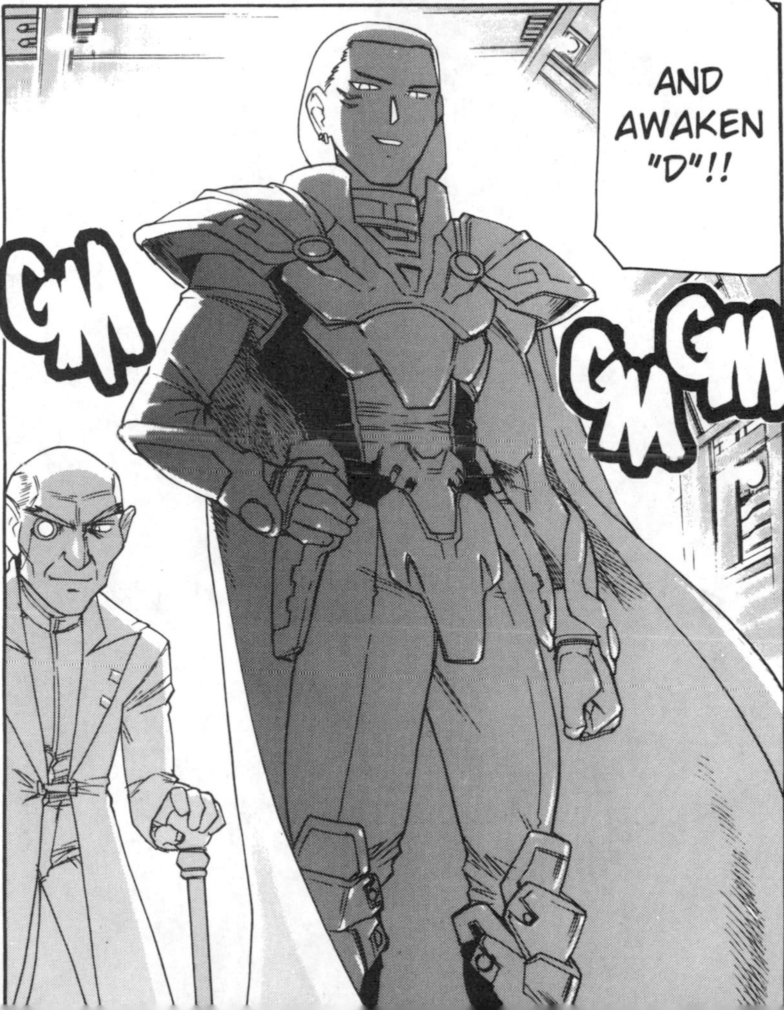
AND AWAKEN "D"!!
GM
GM GM

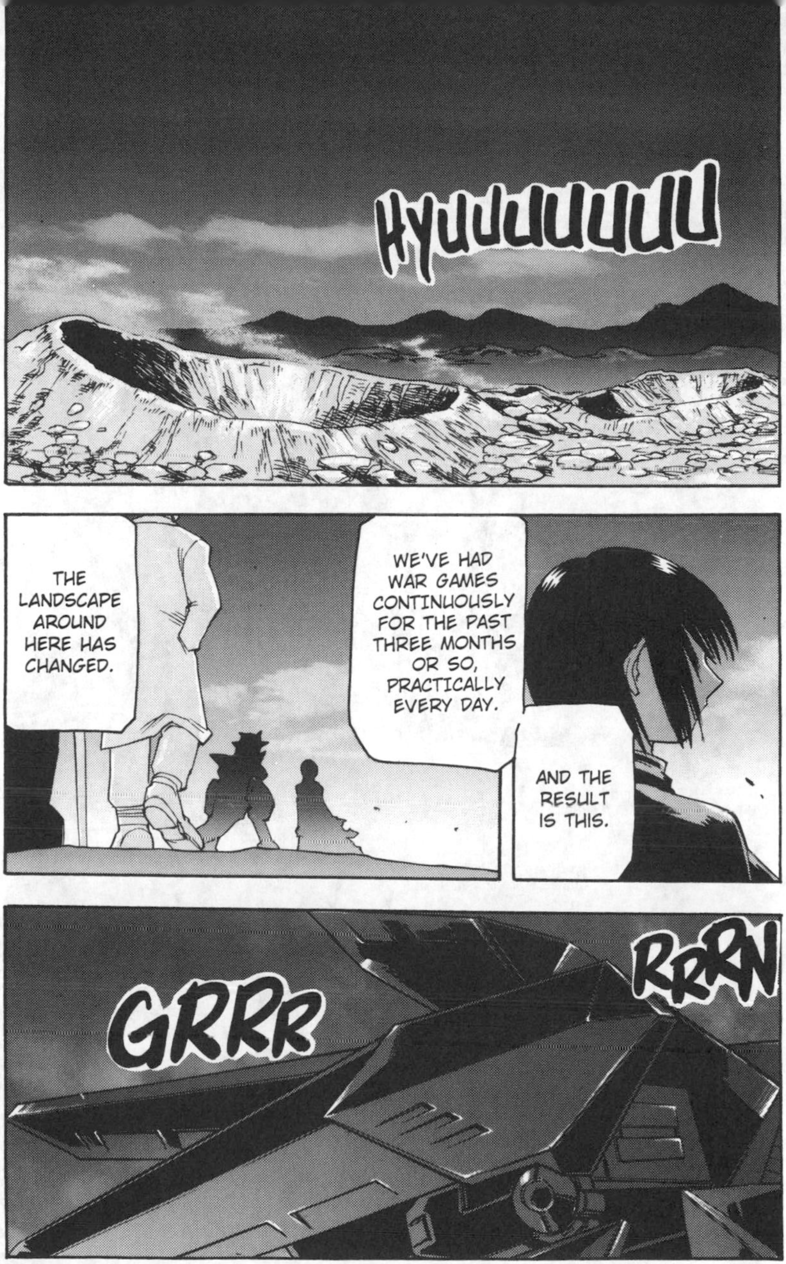
HYUUUUUUU
THE LANDSCAPE AROUND HERE HAS CHANGED.
WE'VE HAD WAR GAMES CONTINUOUSLY FOR THE PAST THREE MONTHS OR SO, PRACTICALLY EVERY DAY.
AND THE RESULT IS THIS.
GRRR
RRRN

Crossing Destinies

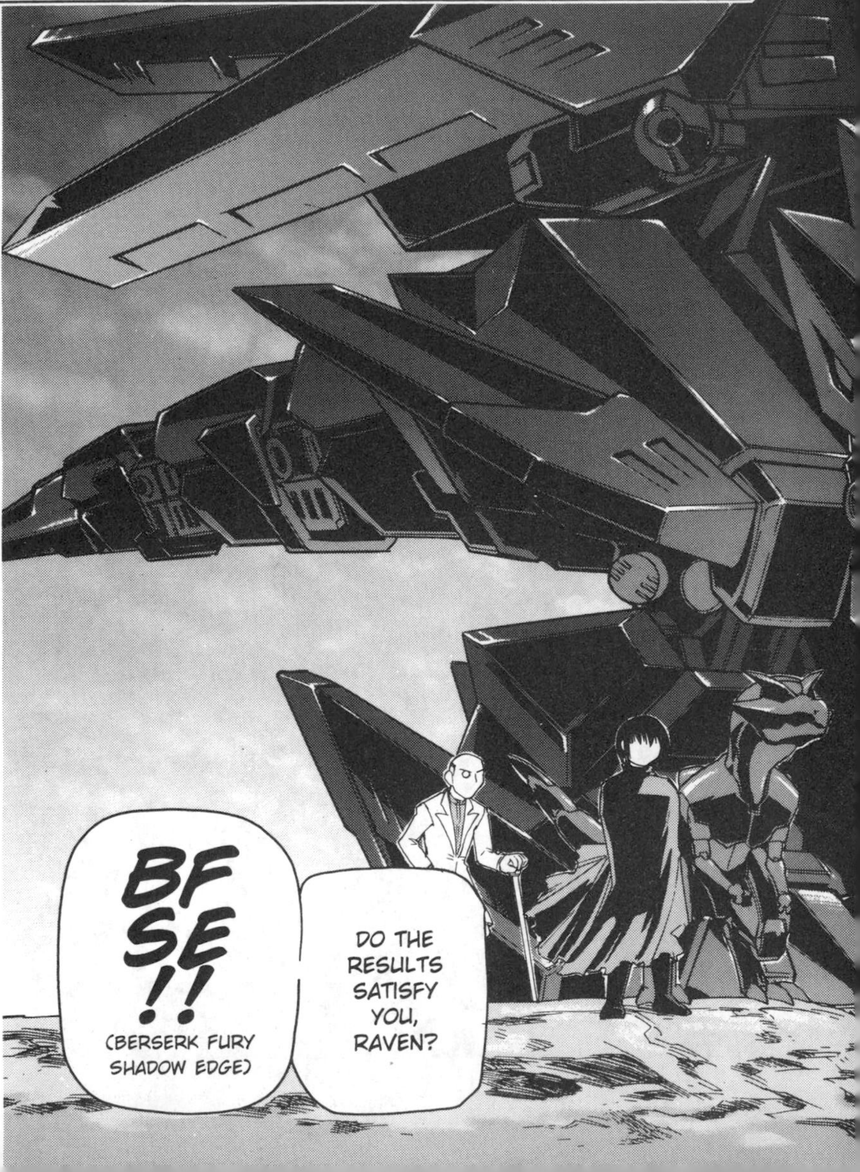
BF SE!!
(BERSERK FURY SHADOW EDGE)
DO THE RESULTS SATISFY YOU, RAVEN?

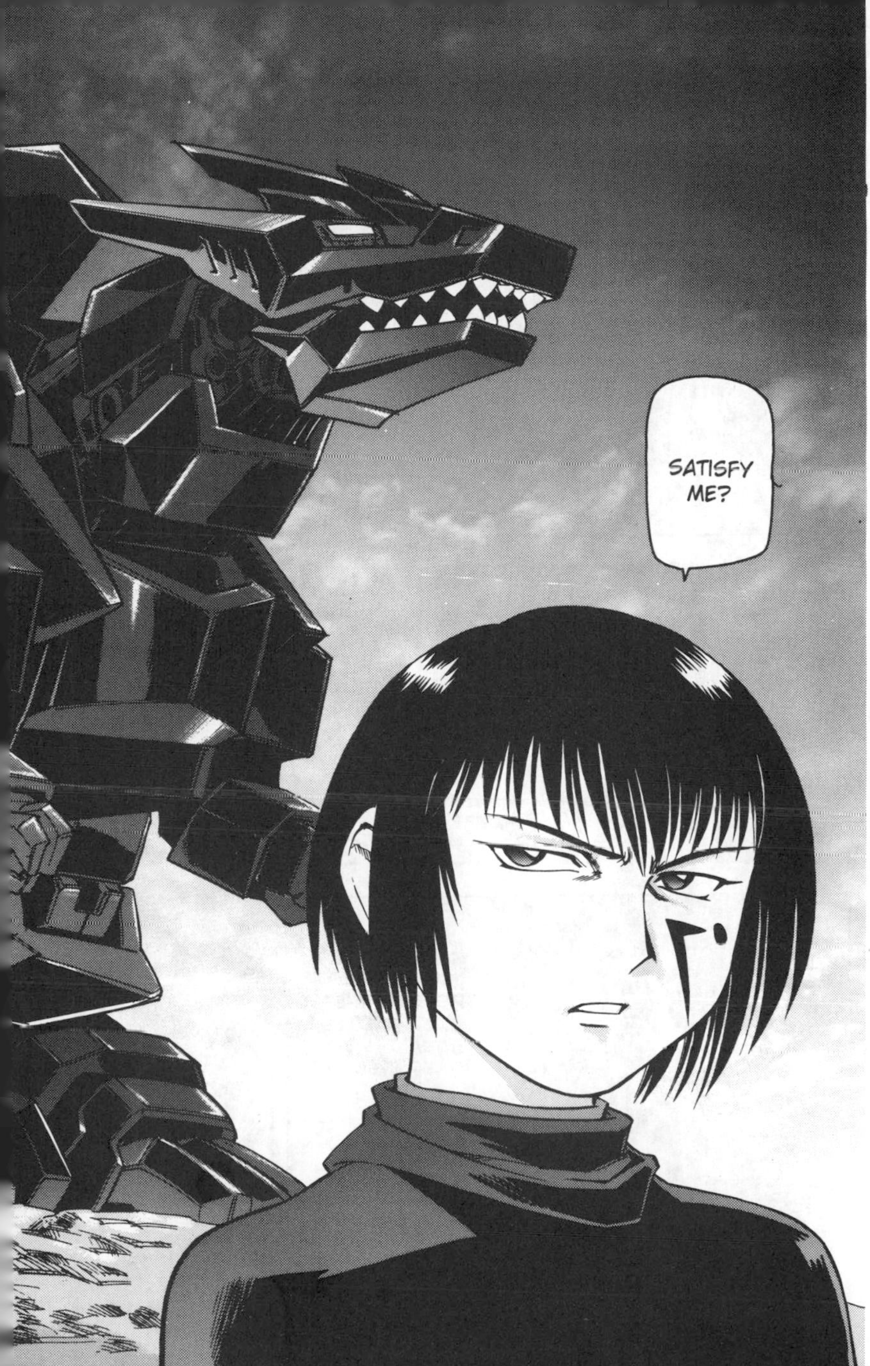
SATISFY ME?

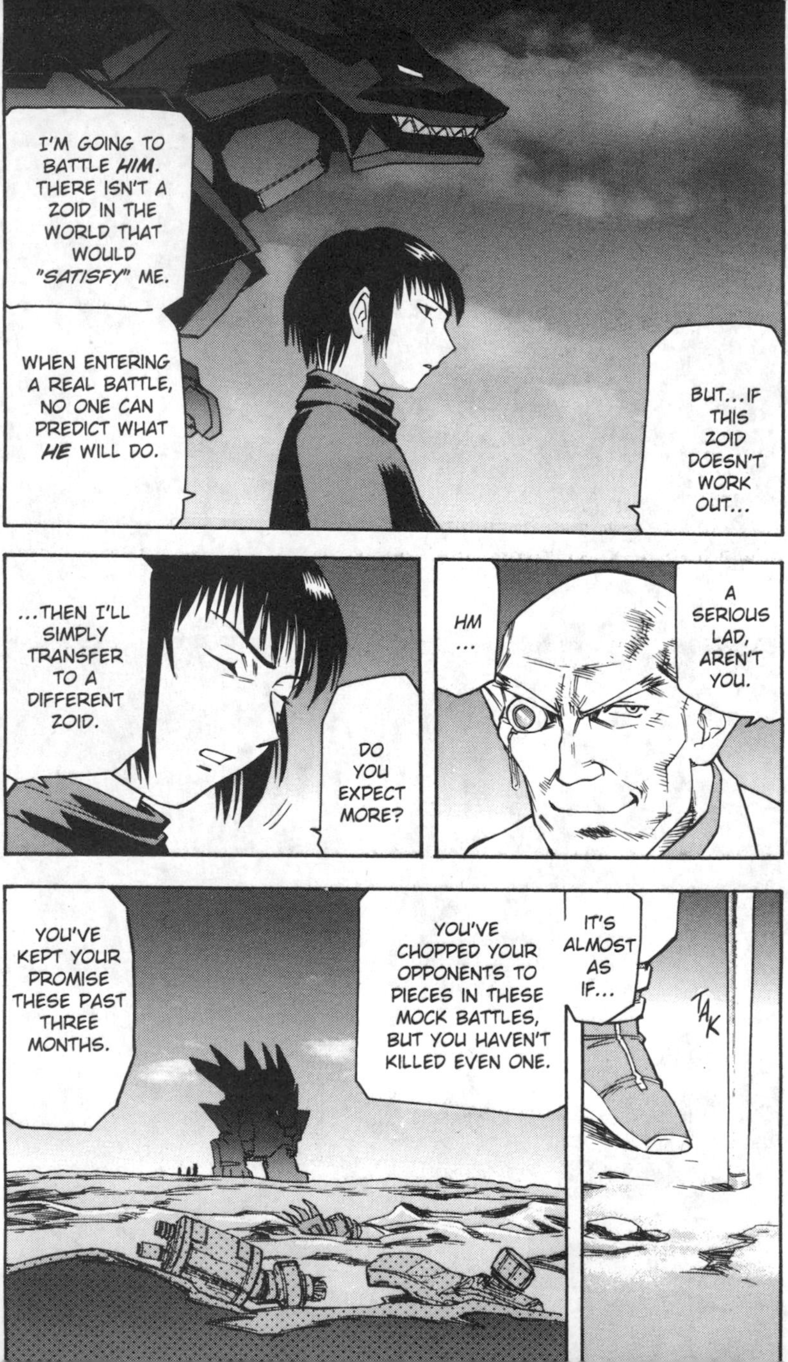

I'M GOING TO BATTLE *HIM*. THERE ISN'T A ZOID IN THE WORLD THAT WOULD "*SATISFY*" ME.
WHEN ENTERING A REAL BATTLE, NO ONE CAN PREDICT WHAT *HE* WILL DO.
BUT...IF THIS ZOID DOESN'T WORK OUT...
...THEN I'LL SIMPLY TRANSFER TO A DIFFERENT ZOID.
DO YOU EXPECT MORE?
HM ...
A SERIOUS LAD, AREN'T YOU.
YOU'VE KEPT YOUR PROMISE THESE PAST THREE MONTHS.
YOU'VE CHOPPED YOUR OPPONENTS TO PIECES IN THESE MOCK BATTLES, BUT YOU HAVEN'T KILLED EVEN ONE.
IT'S ALMOST AS IF...
TAK

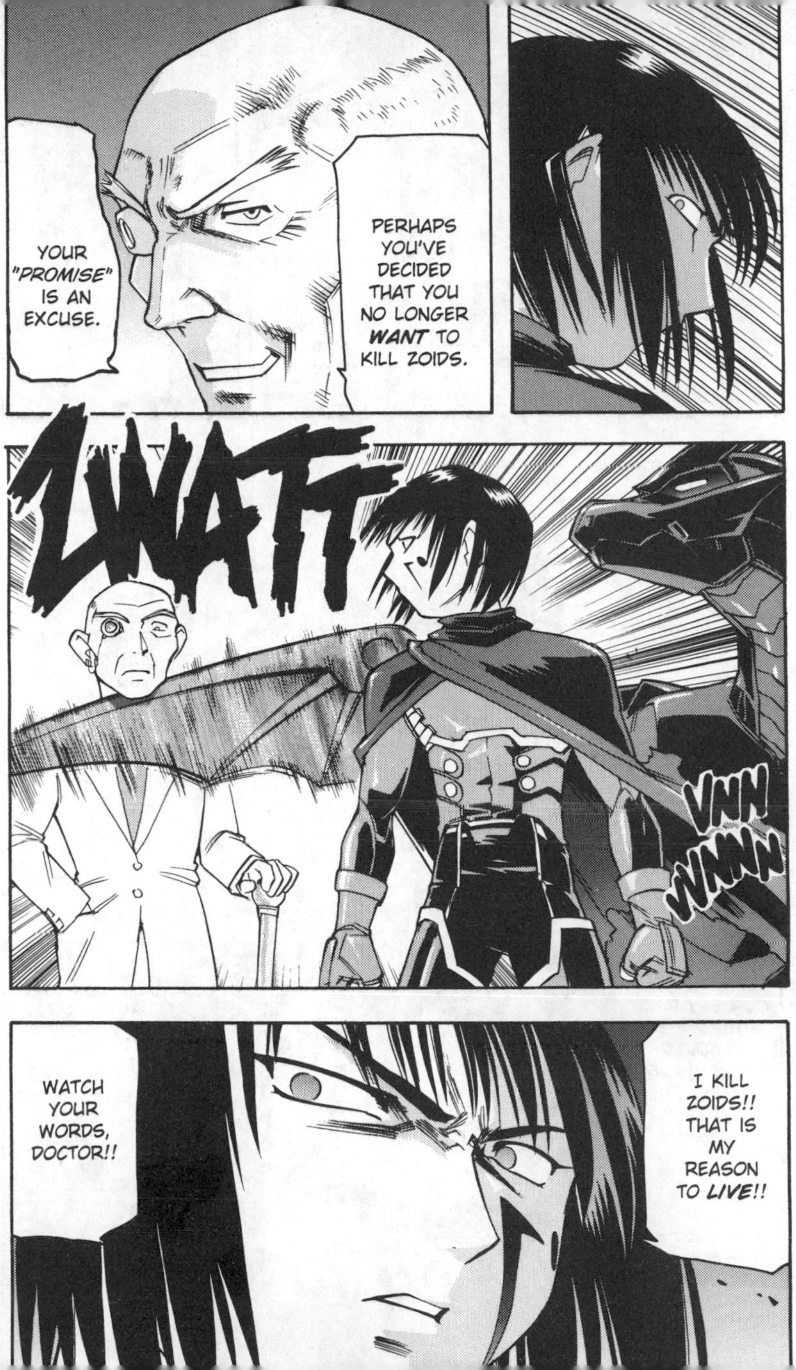
YOUR "PROMISE" IS AN EXCUSE.
PERHAPS YOU'VE DECIDED THAT YOU NO LONGER WANT TO KILL ZOIDS.
ZWATT
VNN VVNNNN
WATCH YOUR WORDS, DOCTOR!!
I KILL ZOIDS!! THAT IS MY REASON TO LIVE!!

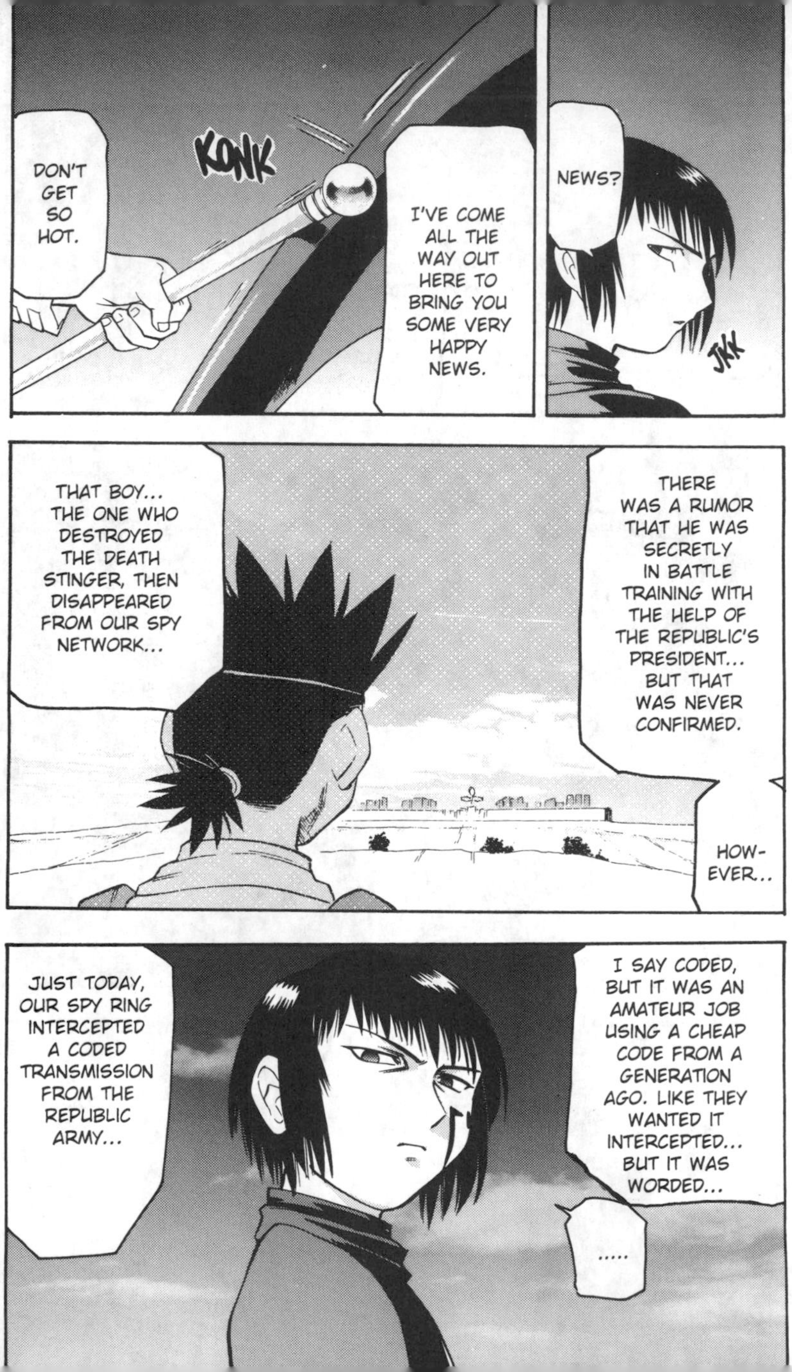
DON'T GET SO HOT.
KONK
I'VE COME ALL THE WAY OUT HERE TO BRING YOU SOME VERY HAPPY NEWS.
NEWS?
JKK
THAT BOY... THE ONE WHO DESTROYED THE DEATH STINGER, THEN DISAPPEARED FROM OUR SPY NETWORK...
THERE WAS A RUMOR THAT HE WAS SECRETLY IN BATTLE TRAINING WITH THE HELP OF THE REPUBLIC'S PRESIDENT... BUT THAT WAS NEVER CONFIRMED.
HOW-EVER...
JUST TODAY, OUR SPY RING INTERCEPTED A CODED TRANSMISSION FROM THE REPUBLIC ARMY...
I SAY CODED, BUT IT WAS AN AMATEUR JOB USING A CHEAP CODE FROM A GENERATION AGO. LIKE THEY WANTED IT INTERCEPTED... BUT IT WAS WORDED...
.....

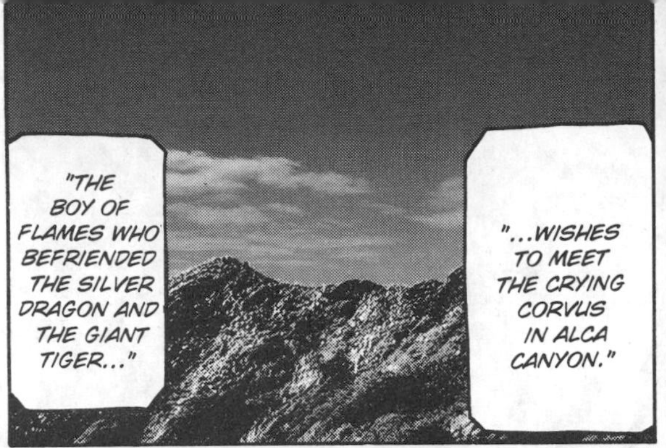
"THE BOY OF FLAMES WHO BEFRIENDED THE SILVER DRAGON AND THE GIANT TIGER..."
"...WISHES TO MEET THE CRYING CORVUS IN ALCA CANYON."
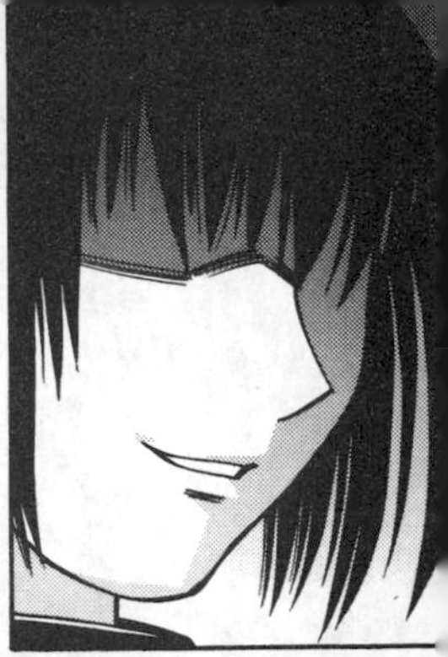

"CORVUS" IS LATIN FOR "RAVEN."

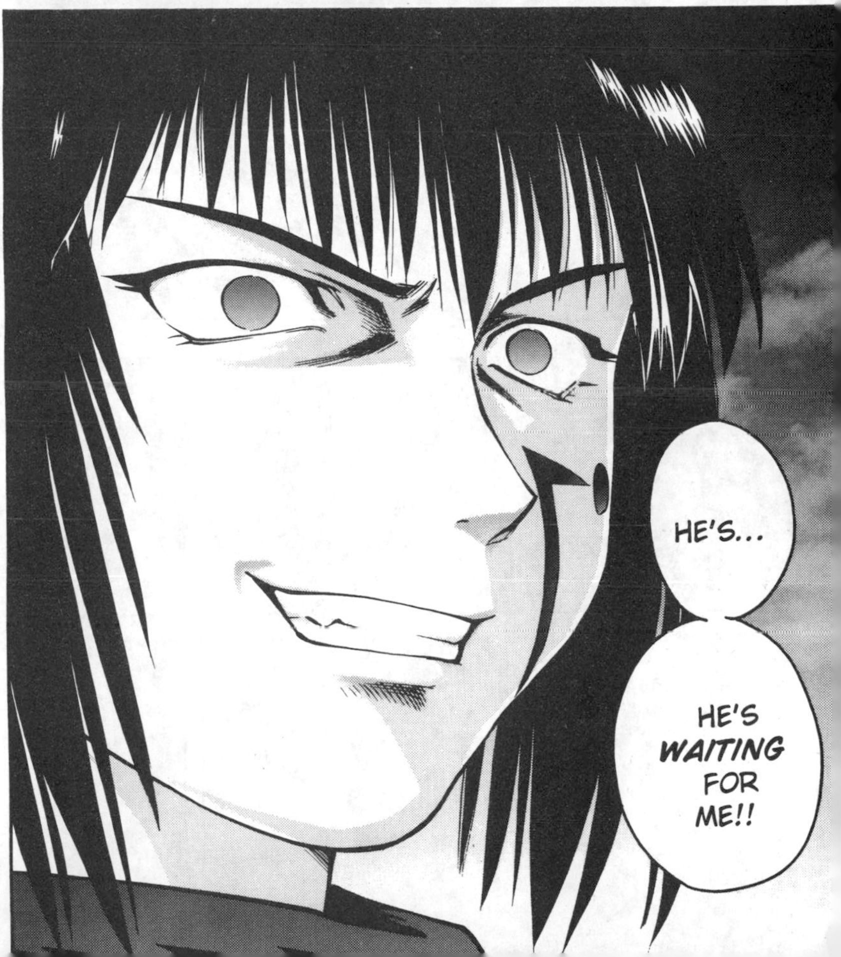
HE'S...
HE'S *WAITING* FOR ME!!

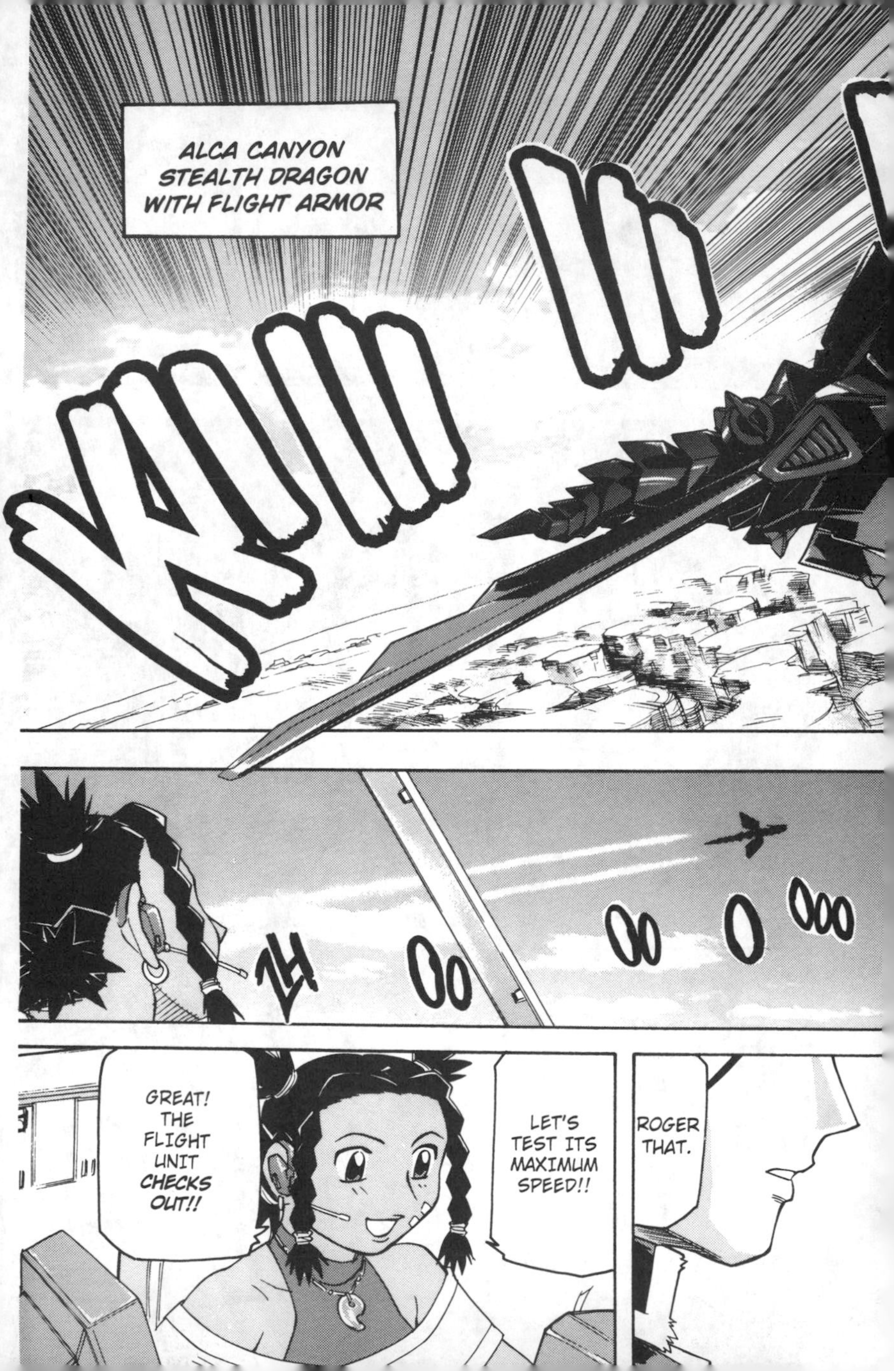
ALCA CANYON
STEALTH DRAGON
WITH FLIGHT ARMOR
KWIIII IIII
GREAT! THE FLIGHT UNIT CHECKS OUT!!
LET'S TEST ITS MAXIMUM SPEED!!
ROGER THAT.

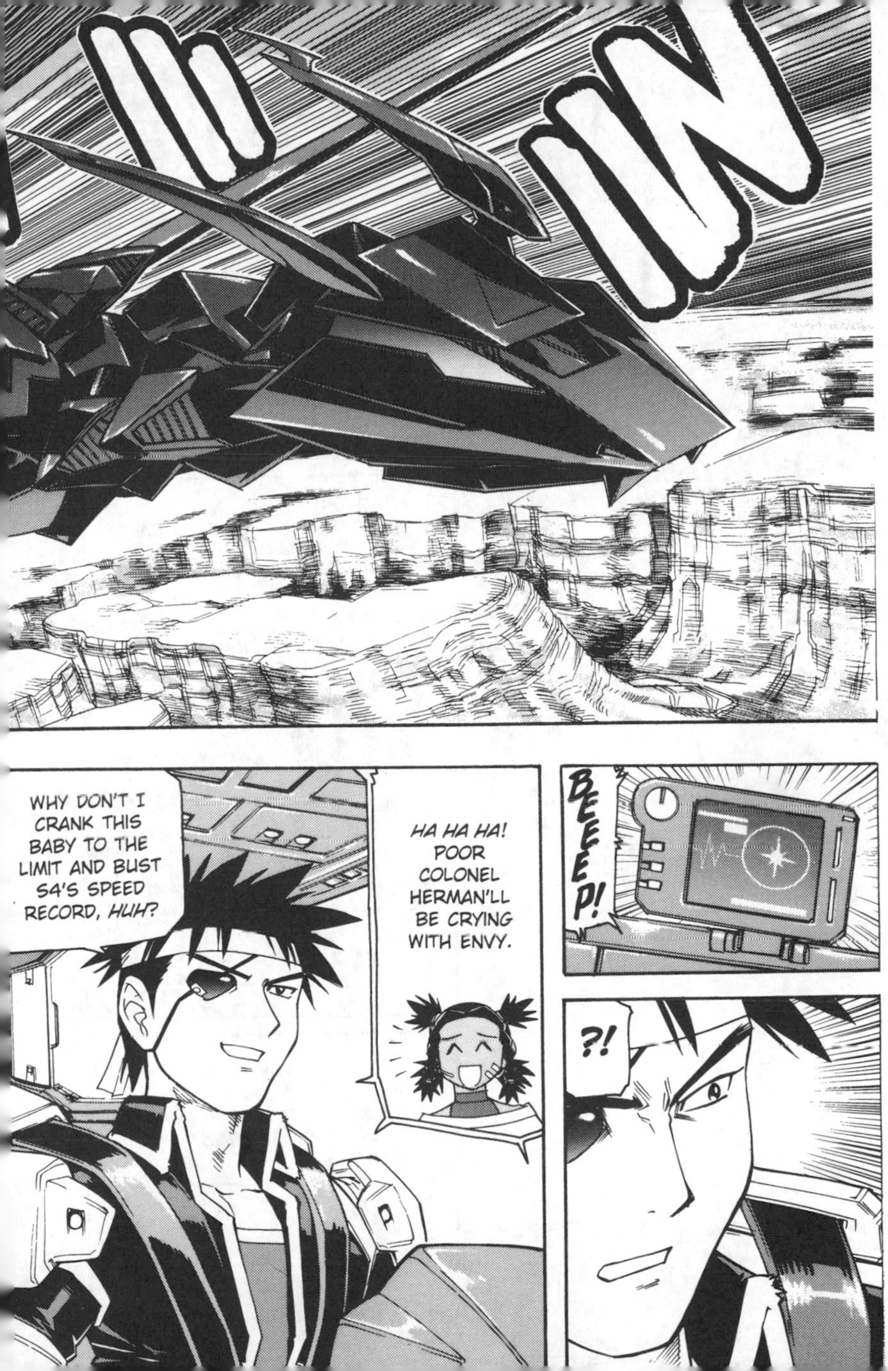
WHY DON'T I CRANK THIS BABY TO THE LIMIT AND BUST S4'S SPEED RECORD, *HUH*?
HA HA HA! POOR COLONEL HERMAN'LL BE CRYING WITH ENVY.
BEEEP!
?!

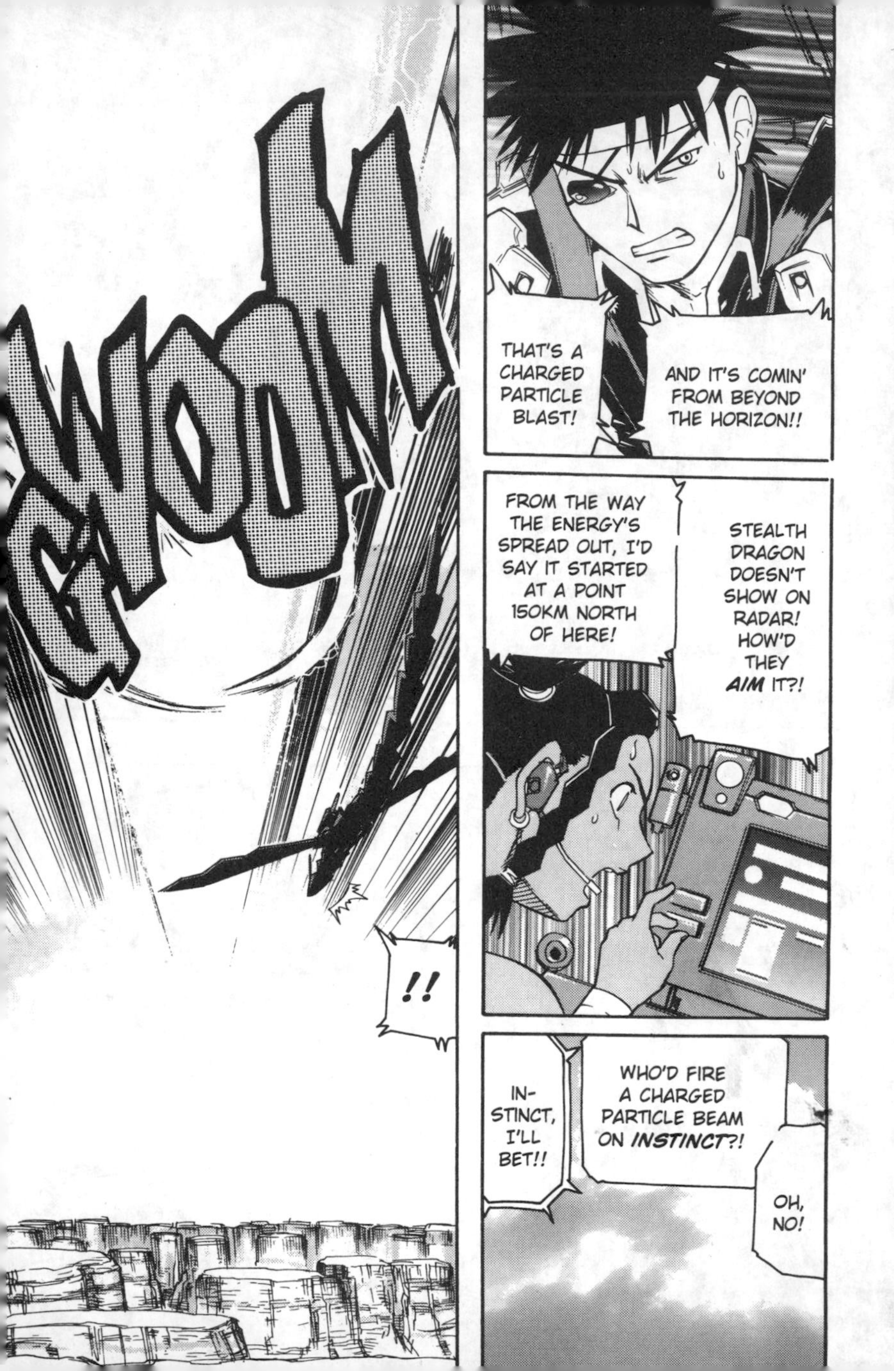
GWOOM
!!
THAT'S A CHARGED PARTICLE BLAST!
AND IT'S COMIN' FROM BEYOND THE HORIZON!!
FROM THE WAY THE ENERGY'S SPREAD OUT, I'D SAY IT STARTED AT A POINT 150KM NORTH OF HERE!
STEALTH DRAGON DOESN'T SHOW ON RADAR! HOW'D THEY *AIM* IT?!
IN-STINCT, I'LL BET!!
WHO'D FIRE A CHARGED PARTICLE BEAM ON *INSTINCT*?!
OH, NO!

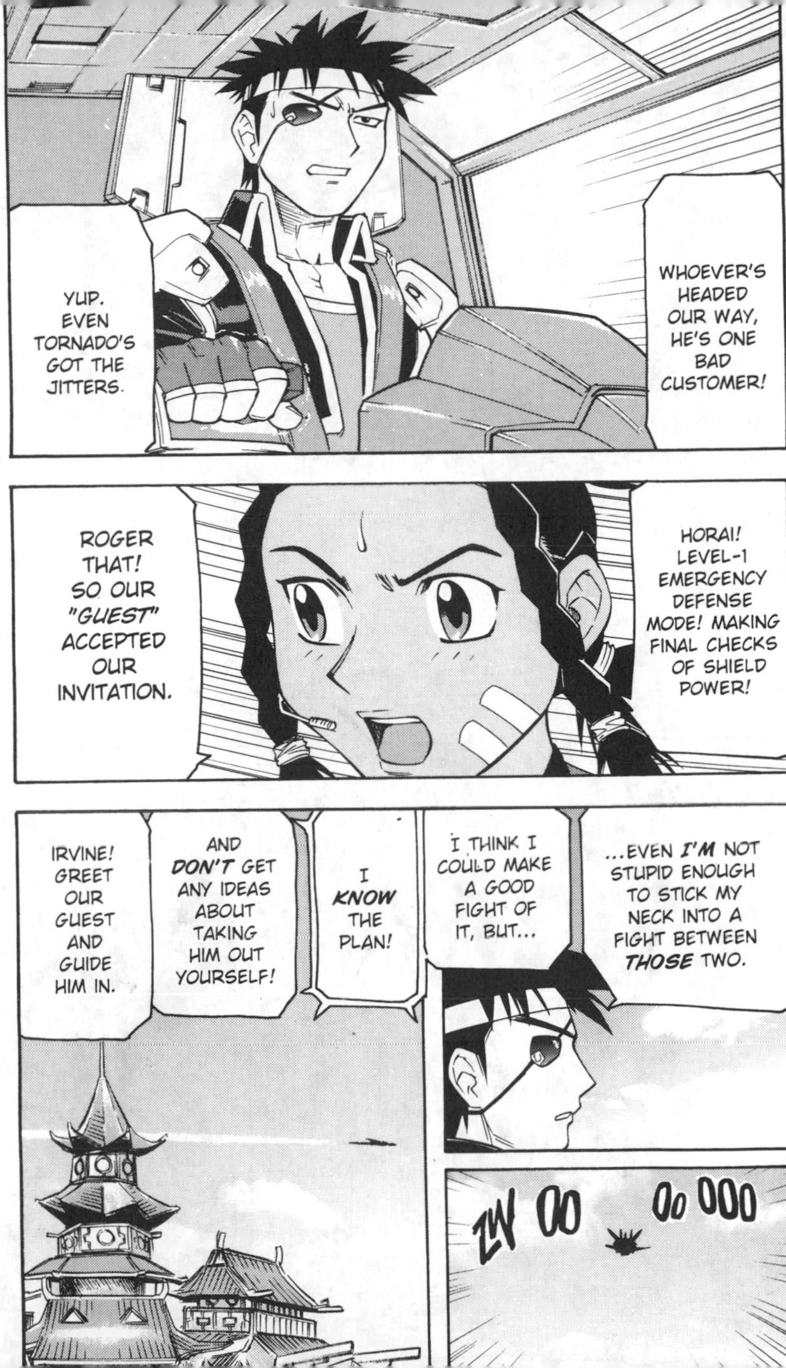
YUP. EVEN TORNADO'S GOT THE JITTERS.
WHOEVER'S HEADED OUR WAY, HE'S ONE BAD CUSTOMER!
ROGER THAT! SO OUR "GUEST" ACCEPTED OUR INVITATION.
HORAI! LEVEL-1 EMERGENCY DEFENSE MODE! MAKING FINAL CHECKS OF SHIELD POWER!
IRVINE! GREET OUR GUEST AND GUIDE HIM IN.
AND DON'T GET ANY IDEAS ABOUT TAKING HIM OUT YOURSELF!
I KNOW THE PLAN!
I THINK I COULD MAKE A GOOD FIGHT OF IT, BUT...
...EVEN I'M NOT STUPID ENOUGH TO STICK MY NECK INTO A FIGHT BETWEEN THOSE TWO.
ZW OO OO OOO

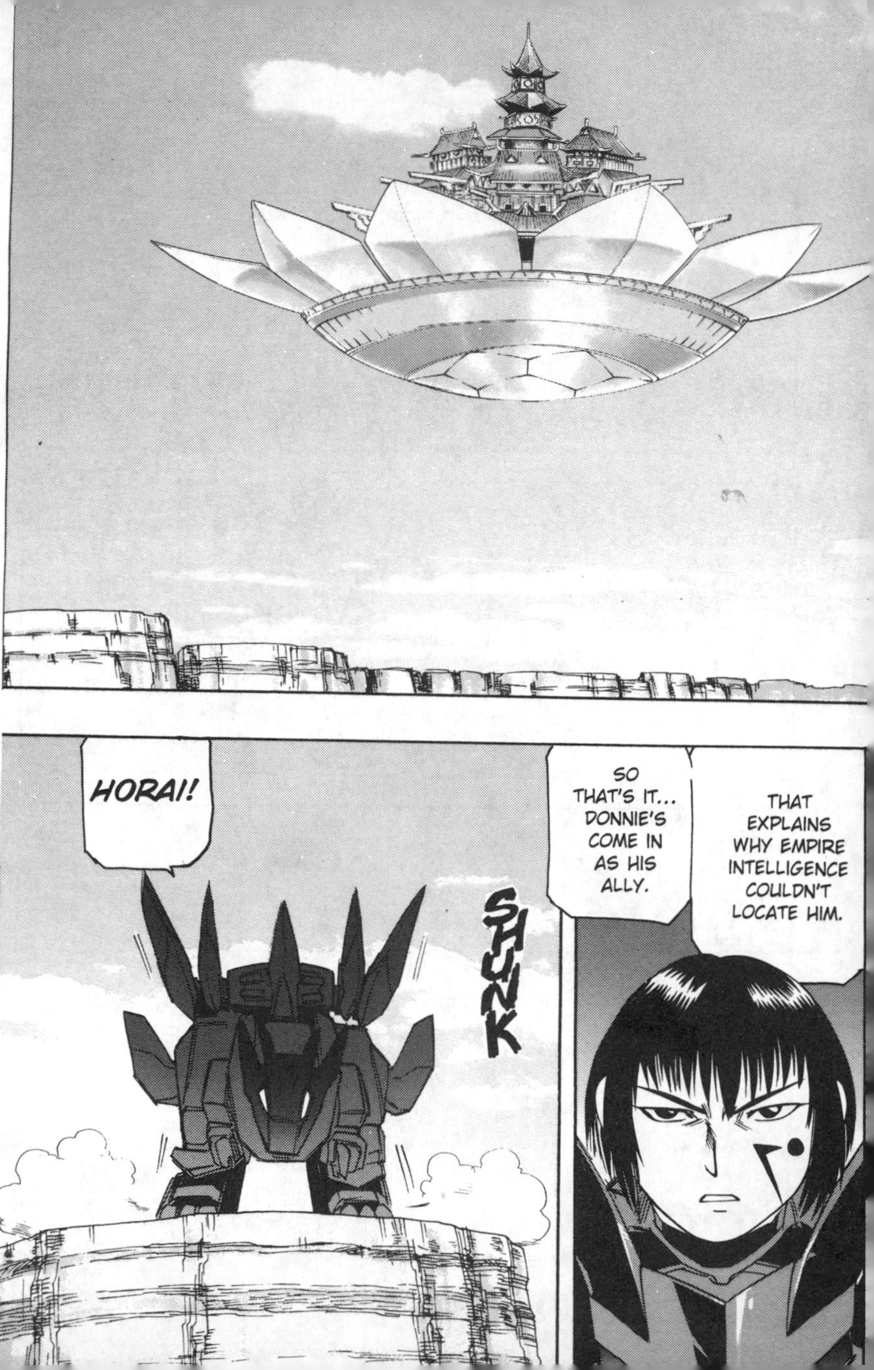
HORAI!
SHUNK
SO THAT'S IT... DONNIE'S COME IN AS HIS ALLY.
THAT EXPLAINS WHY EMPIRE INTELLIGENCE COULDN'T LOCATE HIM.

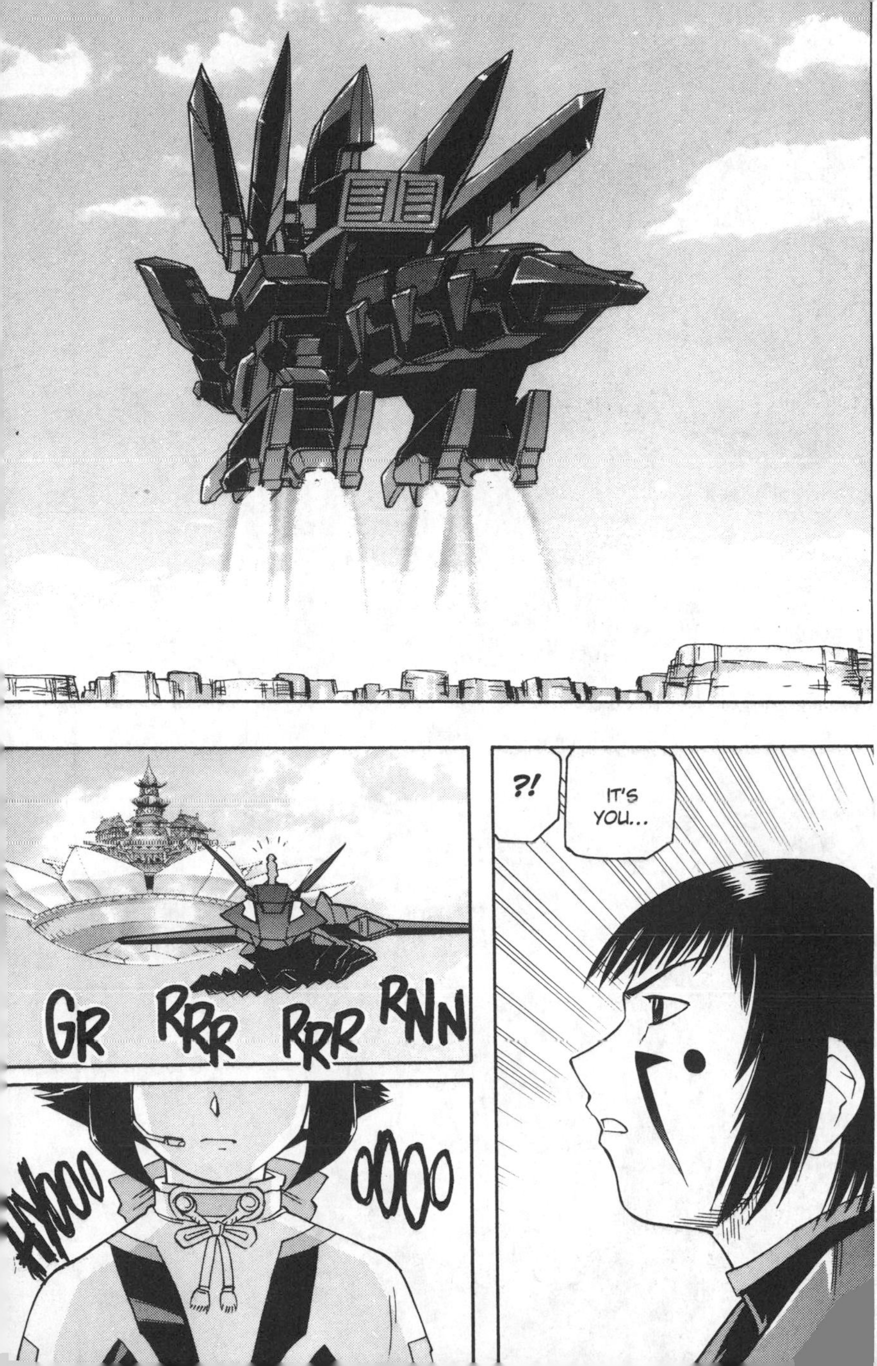
GR RRR RRR RNN
HYOOO OOOO
?!
IT'S YOU...

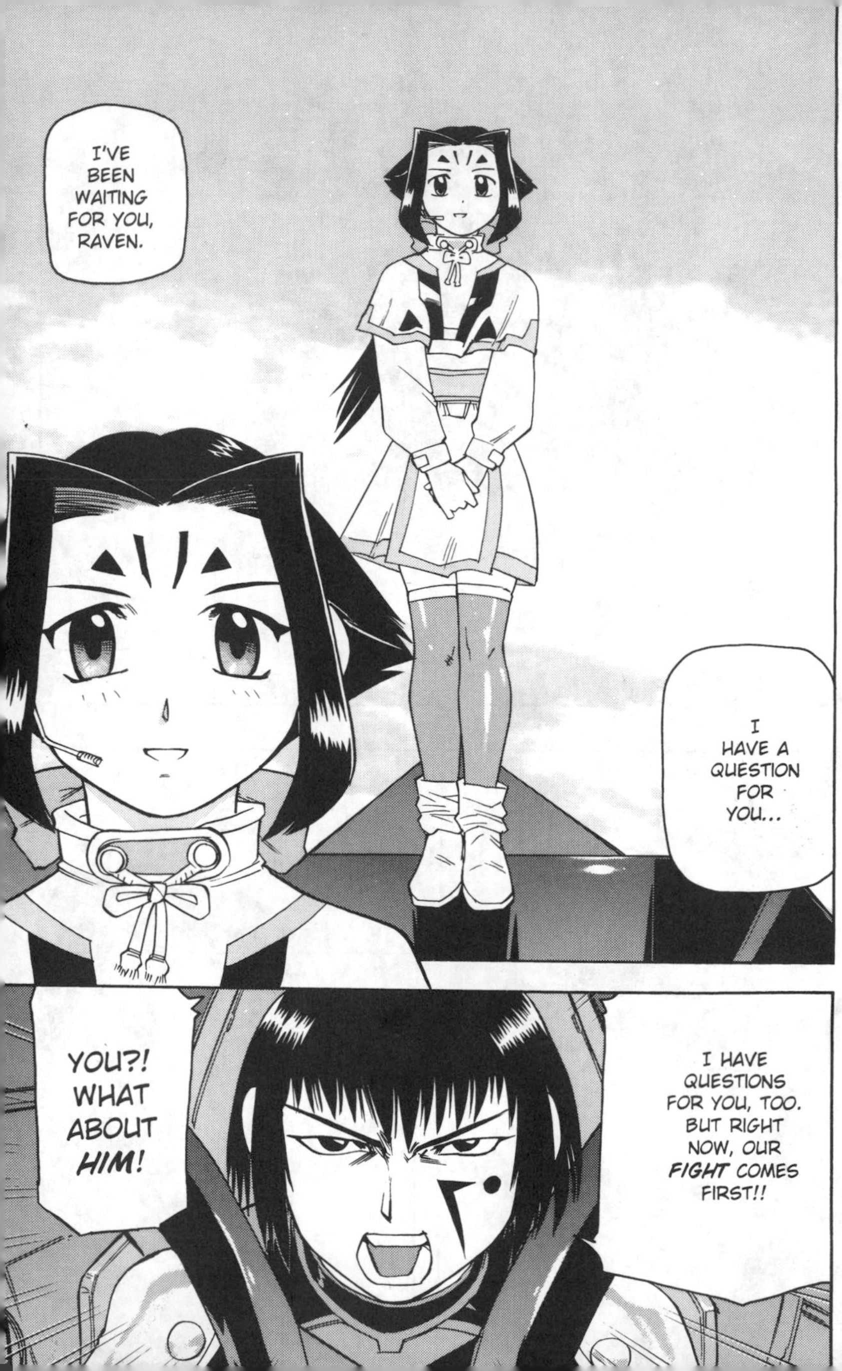
I'VE BEEN WAITING FOR YOU, RAVEN.
I HAVE A QUESTION FOR YOU...
YOU?! WHAT ABOUT *HIM*!
I HAVE QUESTIONS FOR YOU, TOO. BUT RIGHT NOW, OUR *FIGHT* COMES FIRST!!

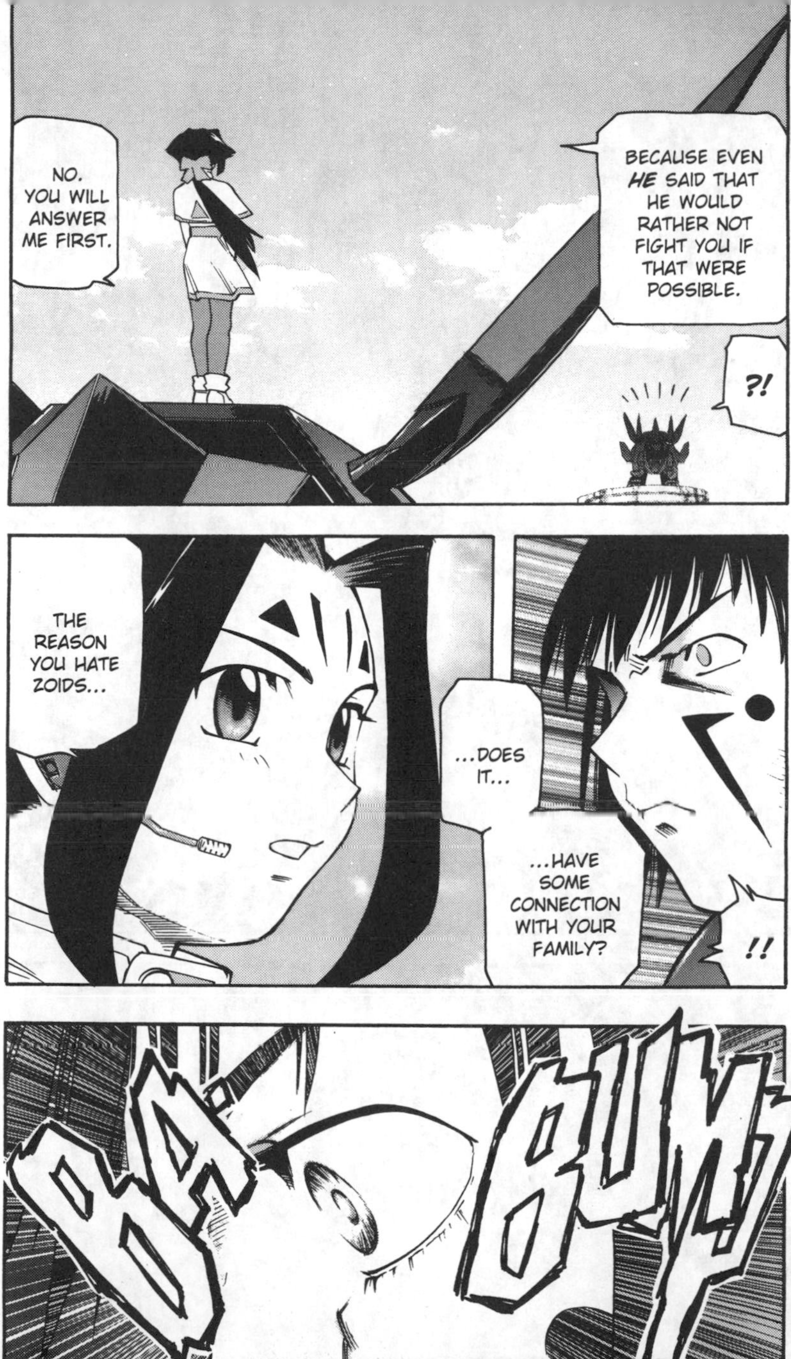
NO. YOU WILL ANSWER ME FIRST.
BECAUSE EVEN *HE* SAID THAT HE WOULD RATHER NOT FIGHT YOU IF THAT WERE POSSIBLE.
?!
THE REASON YOU HATE ZOIDS...
...DOES IT...
...HAVE SOME CONNECTION WITH YOUR FAMILY?
!!
BA BUM!

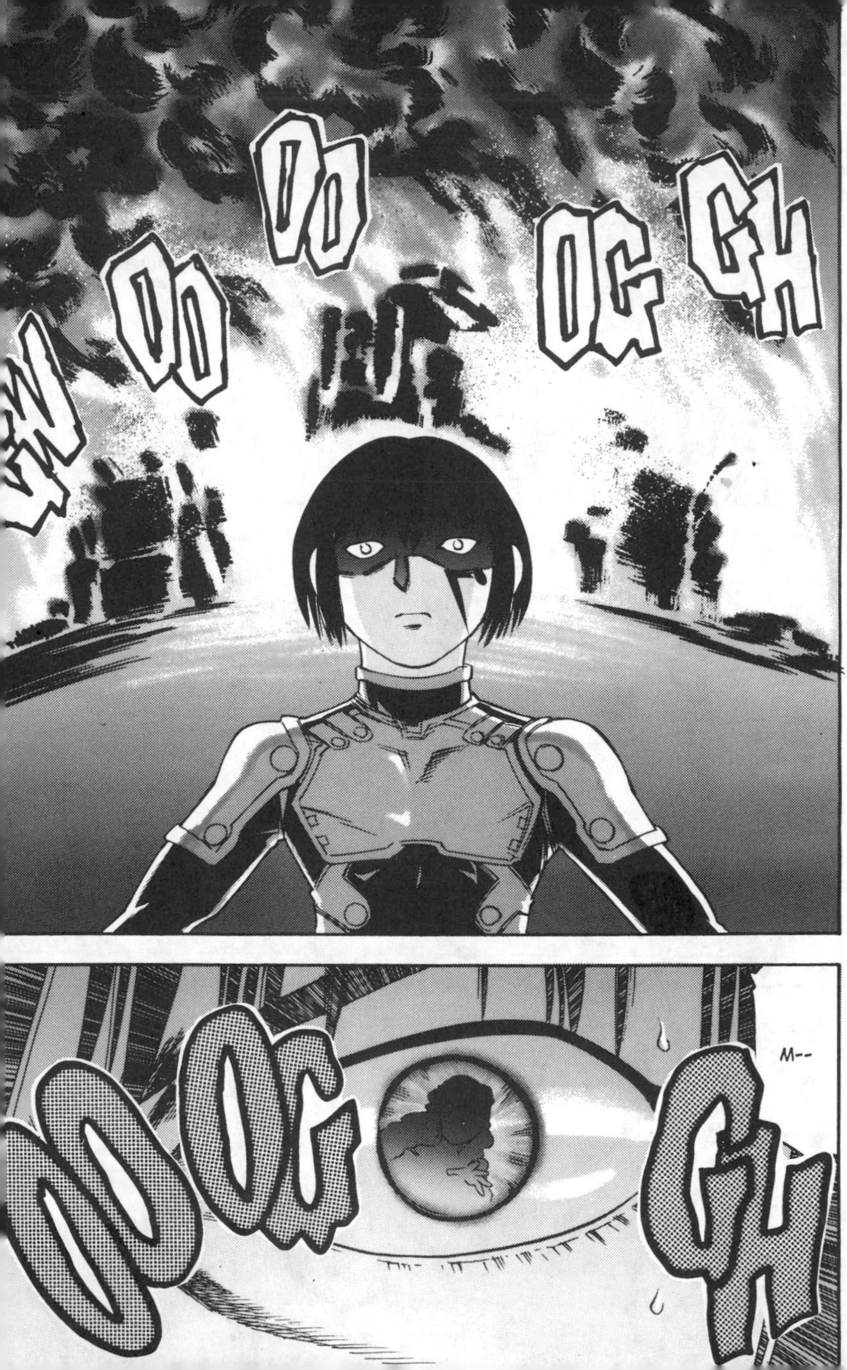
GWOOOOOOGH
OOOGGH
M--

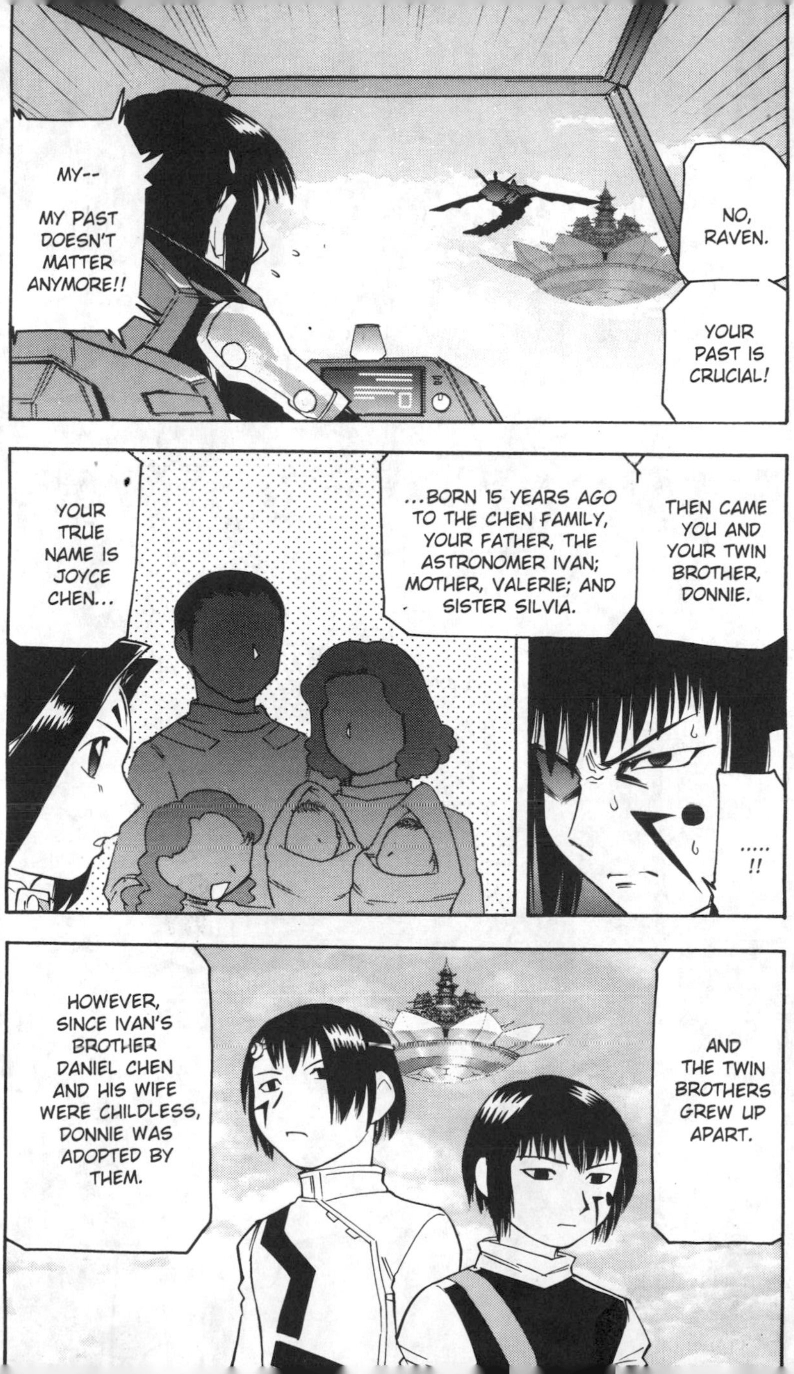
MY--
MY PAST DOESN'T MATTER ANYMORE!!
NO, RAVEN.
YOUR PAST IS CRUCIAL!
YOUR TRUE NAME IS JOYCE CHEN...
...BORN 15 YEARS AGO TO THE CHEN FAMILY, YOUR FATHER, THE ASTRONOMER IVAN; MOTHER, VALERIE; AND SISTER SILVIA.
THEN CAME YOU AND YOUR TWIN BROTHER, DONNIE.
.....!!
HOWEVER, SINCE IVAN'S BROTHER DANIEL CHEN AND HIS WIFE WERE CHILDLESS, DONNIE WAS ADOPTED BY THEM.
AND THE TWIN BROTHERS GREW UP APART.

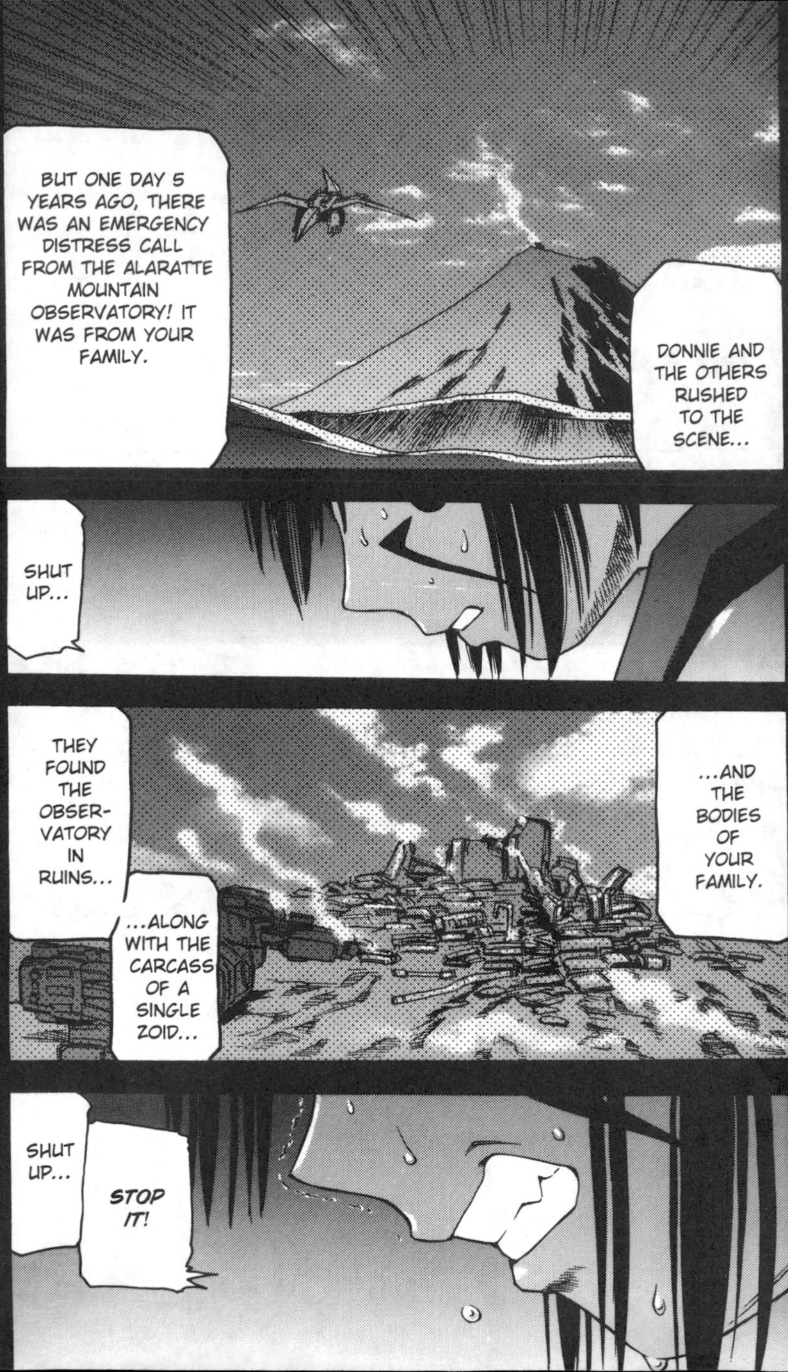
BUT ONE DAY 5 YEARS AGO, THERE WAS AN EMERGENCY DISTRESS CALL FROM THE ALARATTE MOUNTAIN OBSERVATORY! IT WAS FROM YOUR FAMILY.
DONNIE AND THE OTHERS RUSHED TO THE SCENE...
SHUT UP...
THEY FOUND THE OBSER-VATORY IN RUINS...
...ALONG WITH THE CARCASS OF A SINGLE ZOID...
...AND THE BODIES OF YOUR FAMILY.
SHUT UP...
STOP IT!

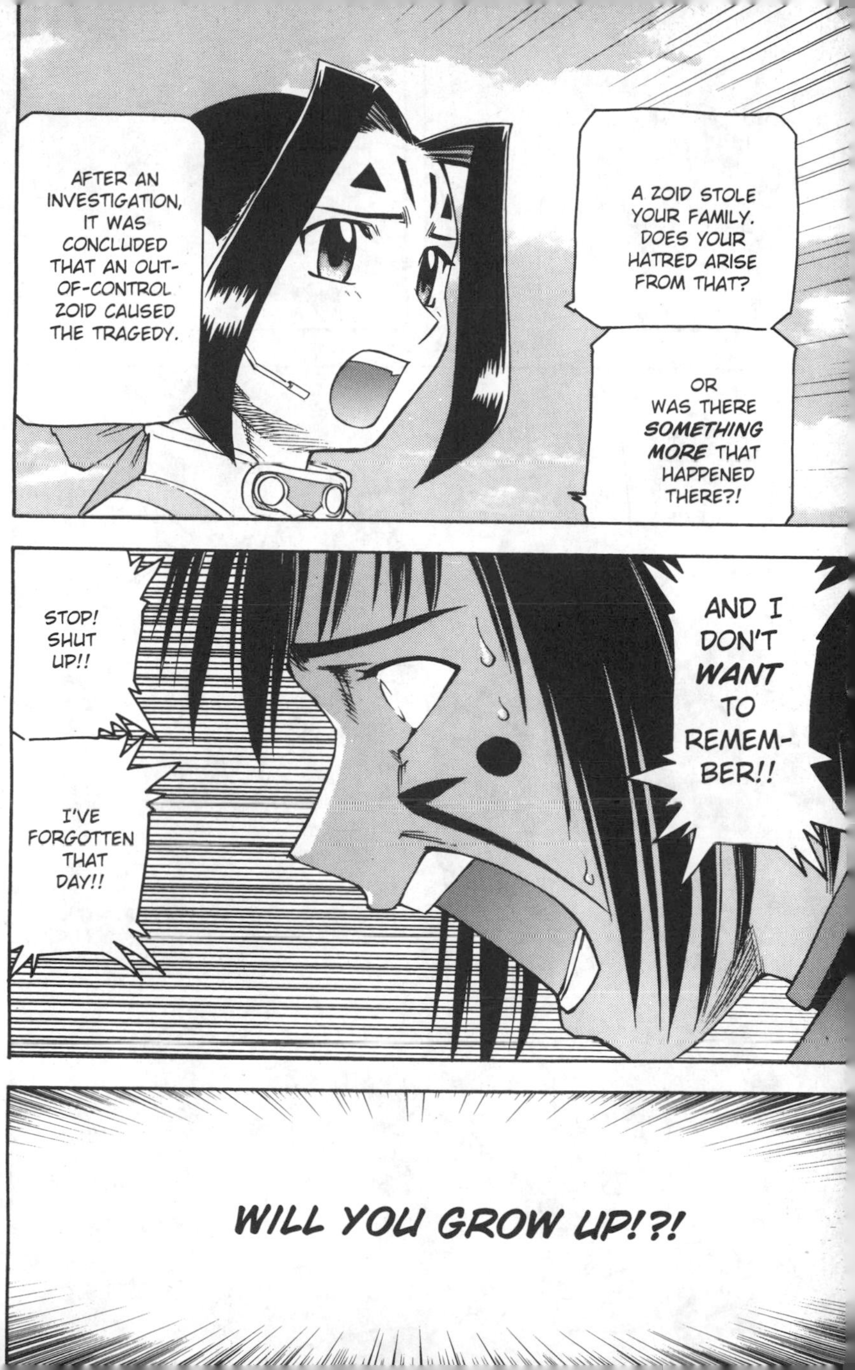
AFTER AN INVESTIGATION, IT WAS CONCLUDED THAT AN OUT-OF-CONTROL ZOID CAUSED THE TRAGEDY.
A ZOID STOLE YOUR FAMILY. DOES YOUR HATRED ARISE FROM THAT?
OR WAS THERE *SOMETHING MORE* THAT HAPPENED THERE?!
STOP! SHUT UP!!
I'VE FORGOTTEN THAT DAY!!
AND I DON'T *WANT* TO REMEMBER!!
WILL YOU GROW UP!?!

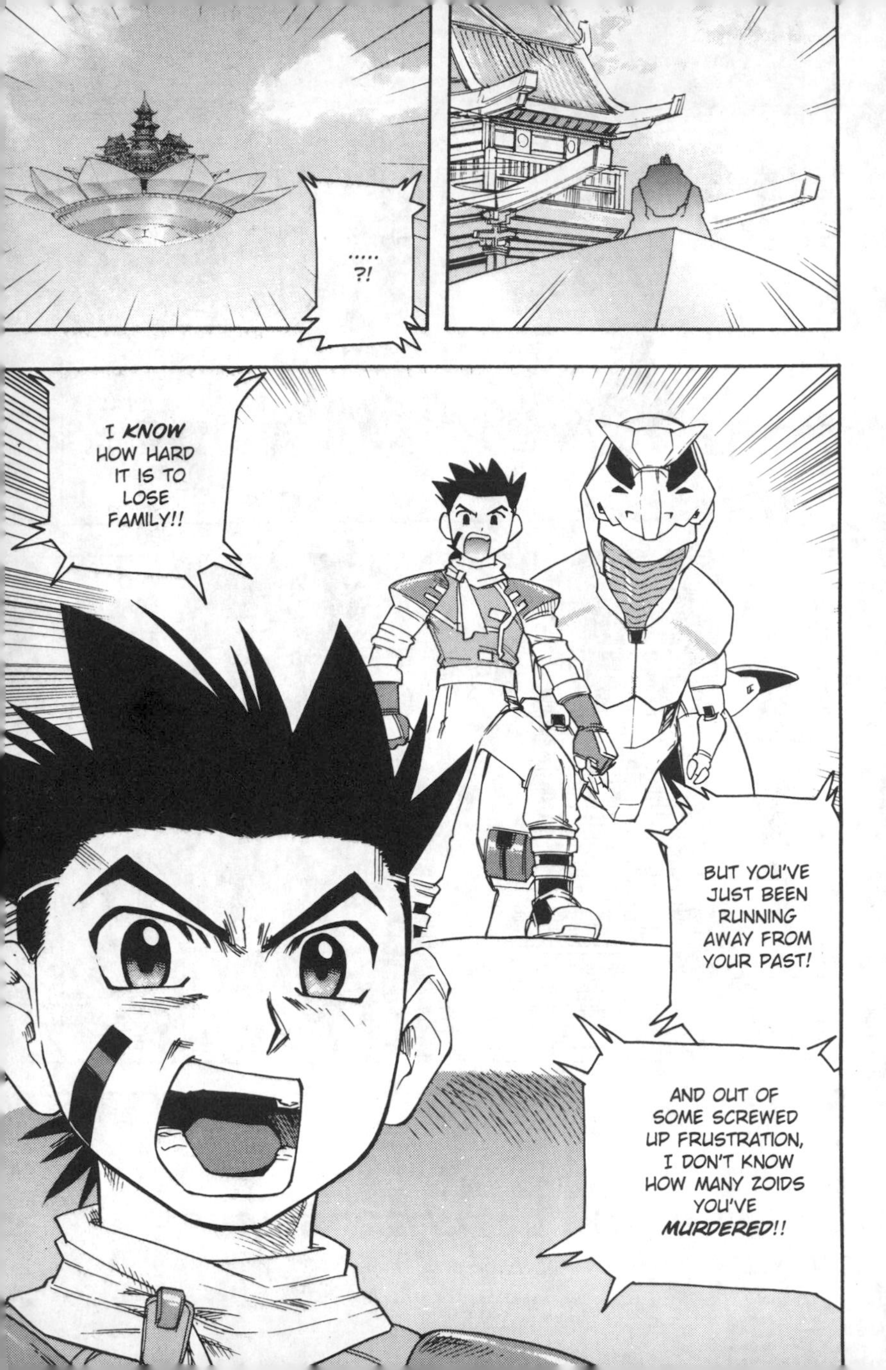
.....
?!
I KNOW HOW HARD IT IS TO LOSE FAMILY!!
BUT YOU'VE JUST BEEN RUNNING AWAY FROM YOUR PAST!
AND OUT OF SOME SCREWED UP FRUSTRATION, I DON'T KNOW HOW MANY ZOIDS YOU'VE MURDERED!!

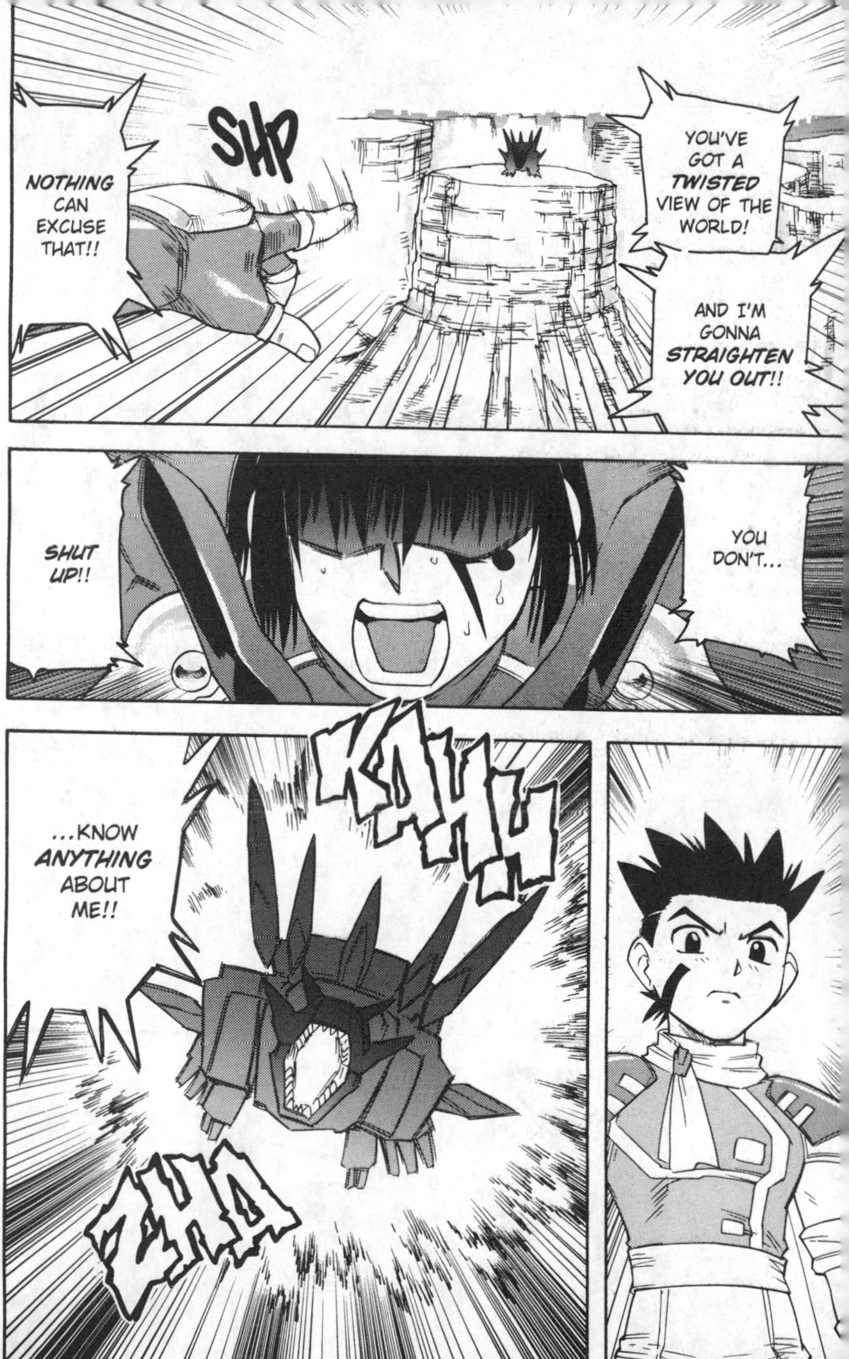
SHP
NOTHING CAN EXCUSE THAT!!
YOU'VE GOT A TWISTED VIEW OF THE WORLD!
AND I'M GONNA STRAIGHTEN YOU OUT!!
SHUT UP!!
YOU DON'T...
...KNOW ANYTHING ABOUT ME!!

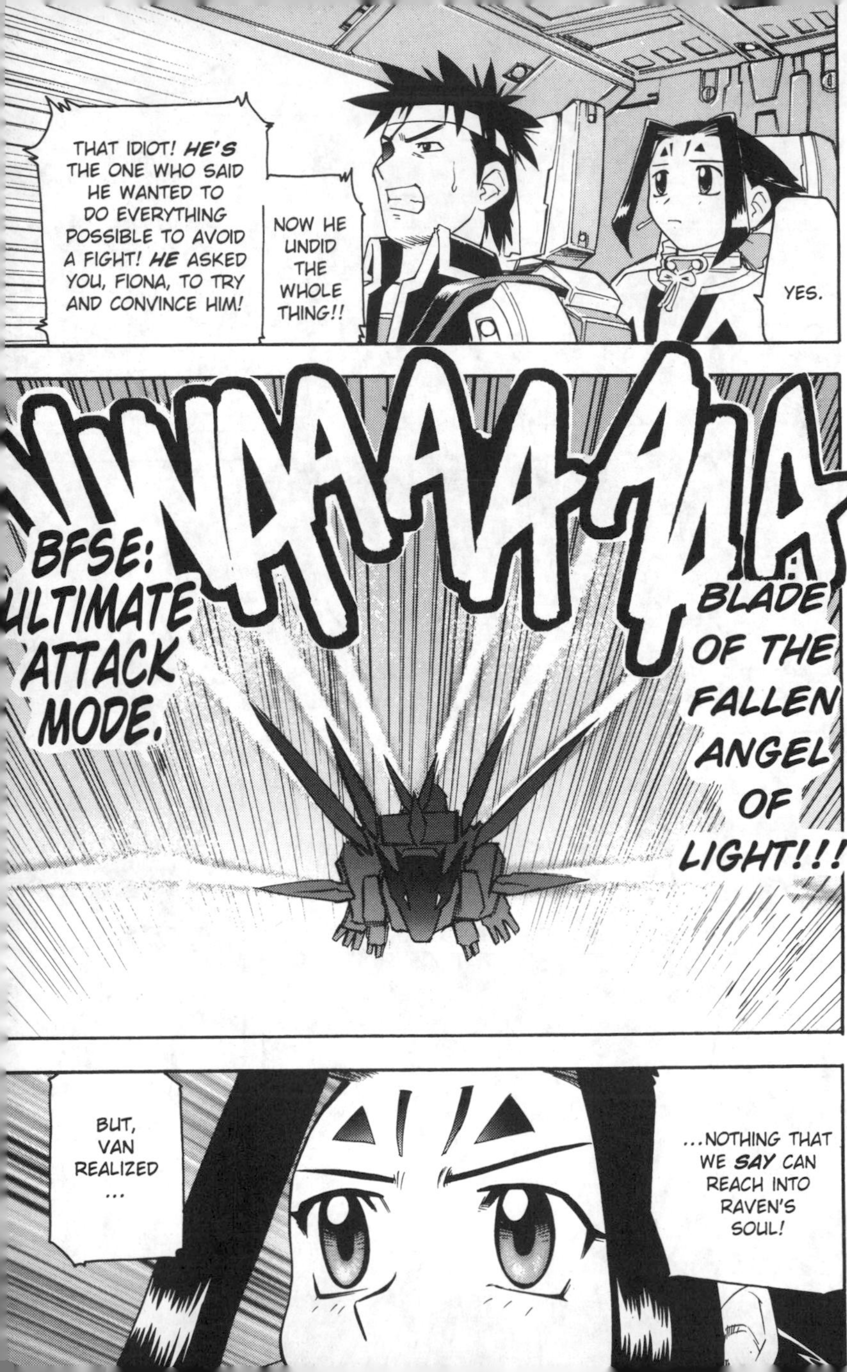
THAT IDIOT! *HE'S* THE ONE WHO SAID HE WANTED TO DO EVERYTHING POSSIBLE TO AVOID A FIGHT! *HE* ASKED YOU, FIONA, TO TRY AND CONVINCE HIM!
NOW HE UNDID THE WHOLE THING!!
YES.
BFSE: ULTIMATE ATTACK MODE.
WAAAAAA
BLADE OF THE FALLEN ANGEL OF LIGHT!!!
BUT, VAN REALIZED ...
...NOTHING THAT WE *SAY* CAN REACH INTO RAVEN'S SOUL!

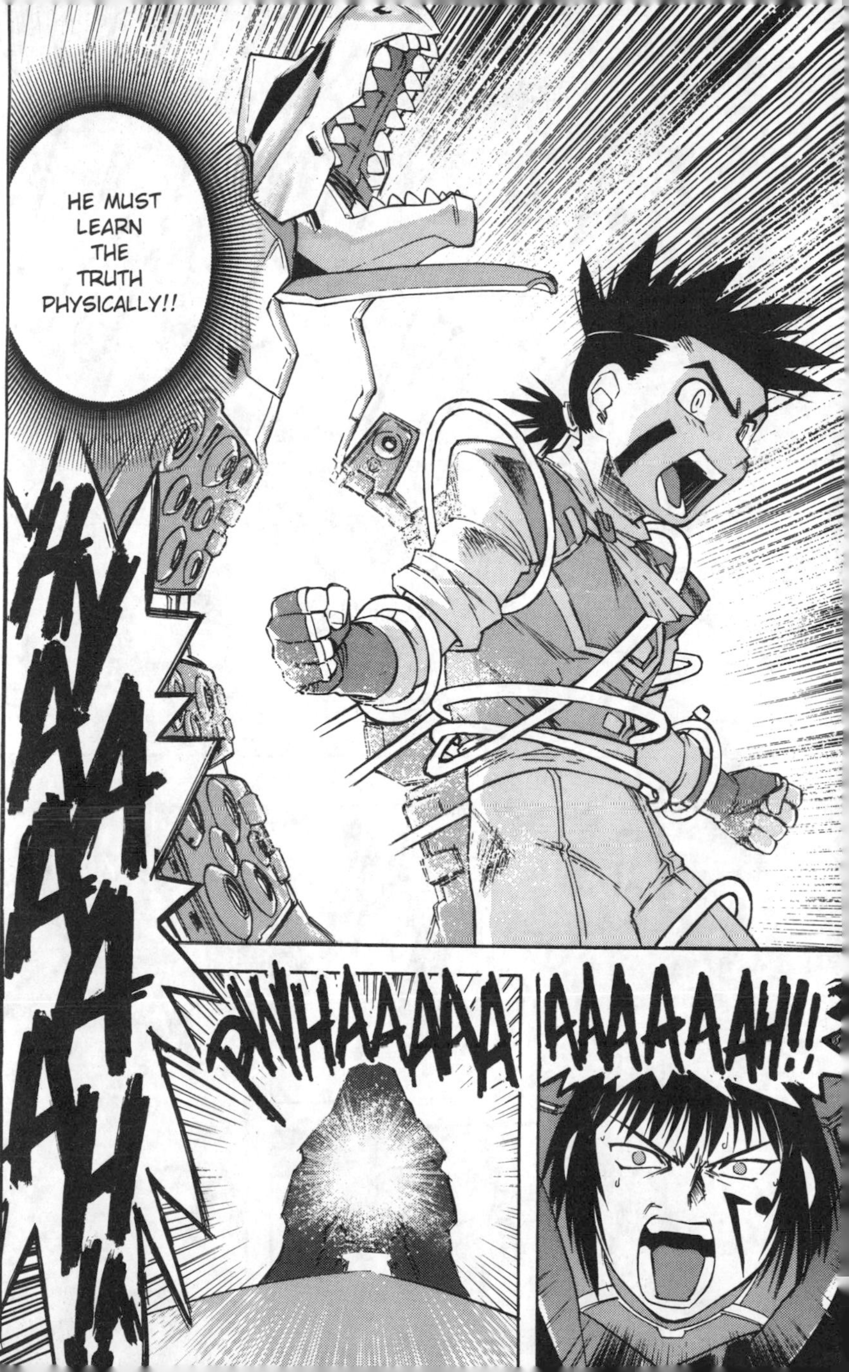
HE MUST LEARN THE TRUTH PHYSICALLY!!
GWHAAAAAA
AAAAAAH!!

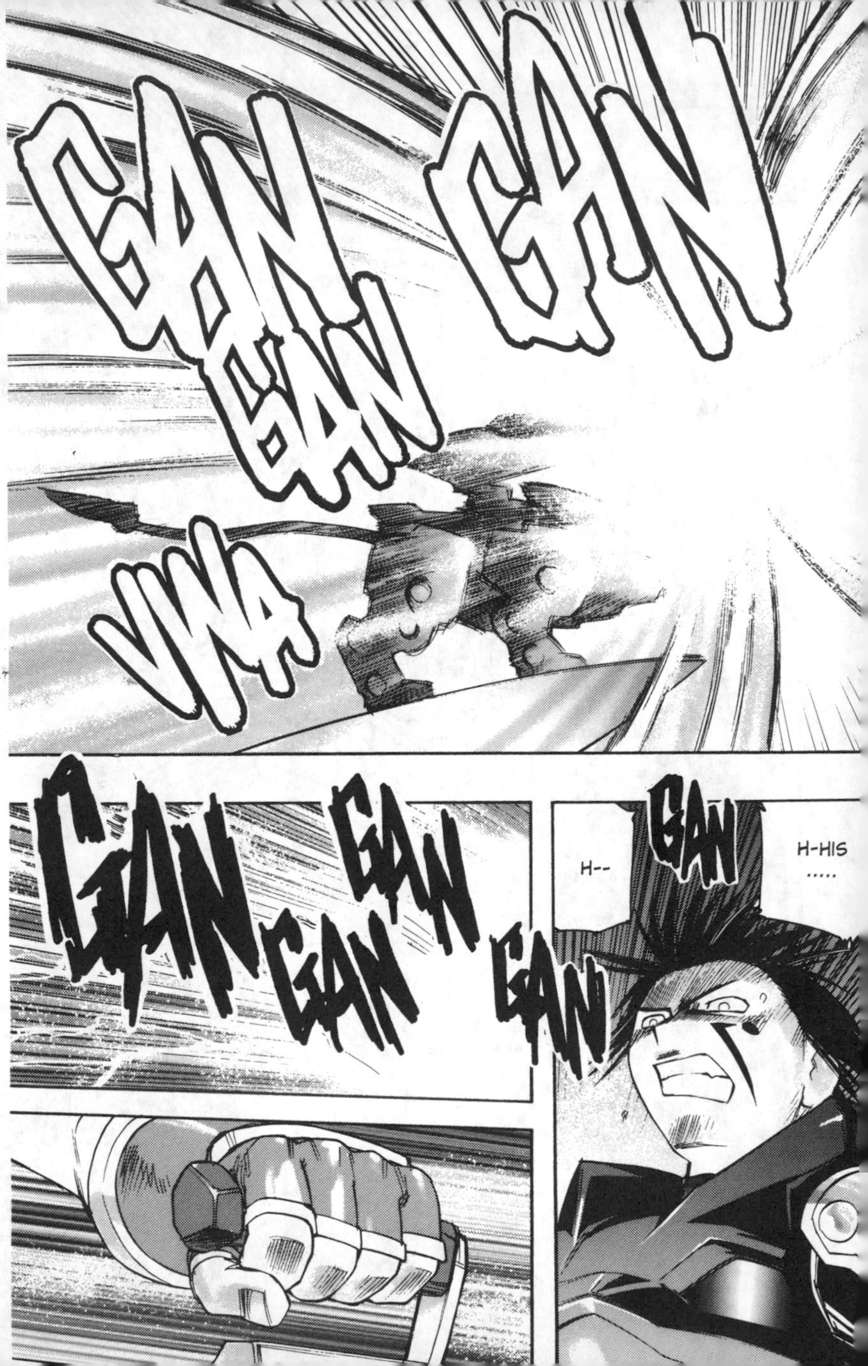
GAN
GAN
GAN
VWA
GAN
GAN
GAN
H--
GAN
H-HIS
.....
GAN

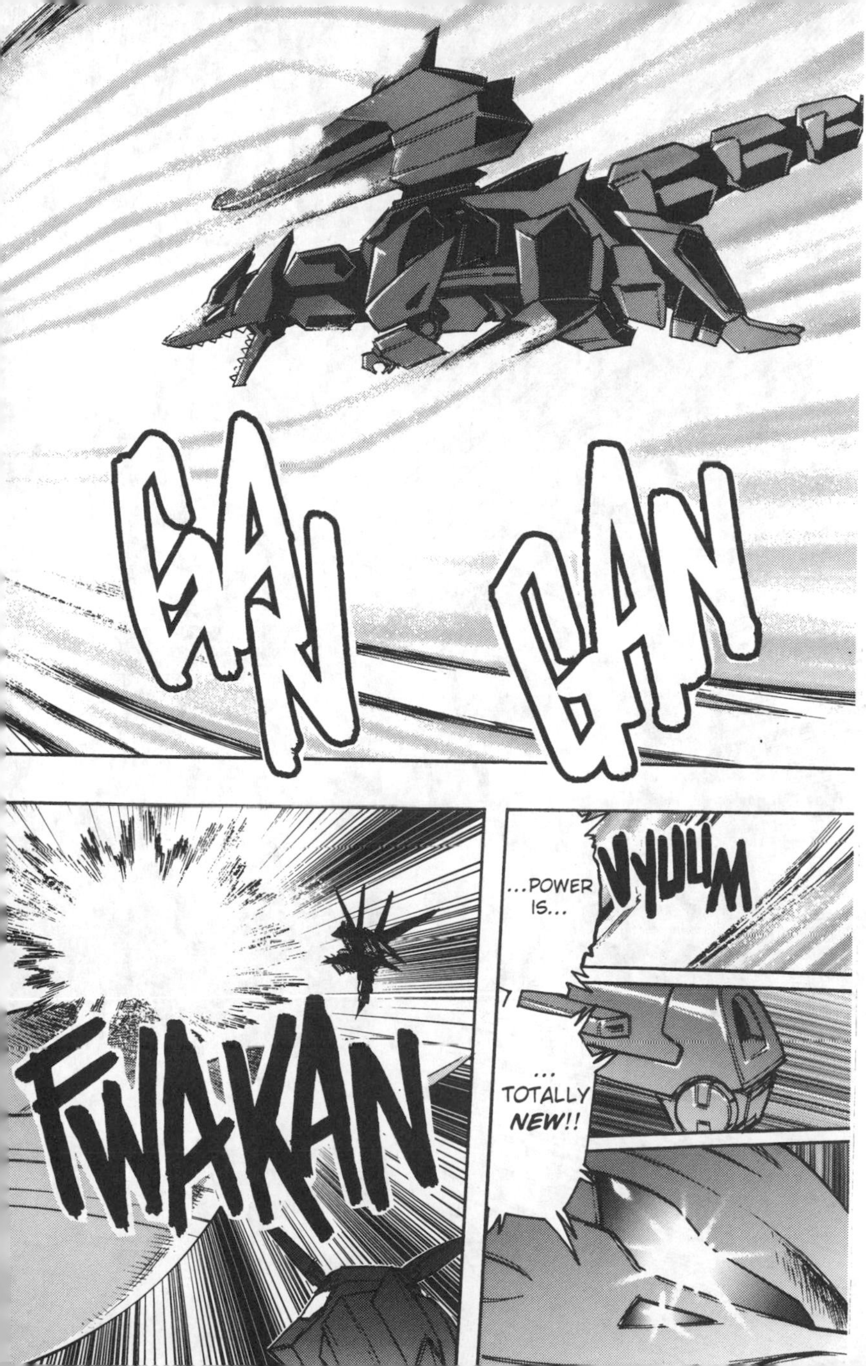
GAN
GAN
FWAKAN
...POWER IS...
VYUUM
... TOTALLY NEW!!

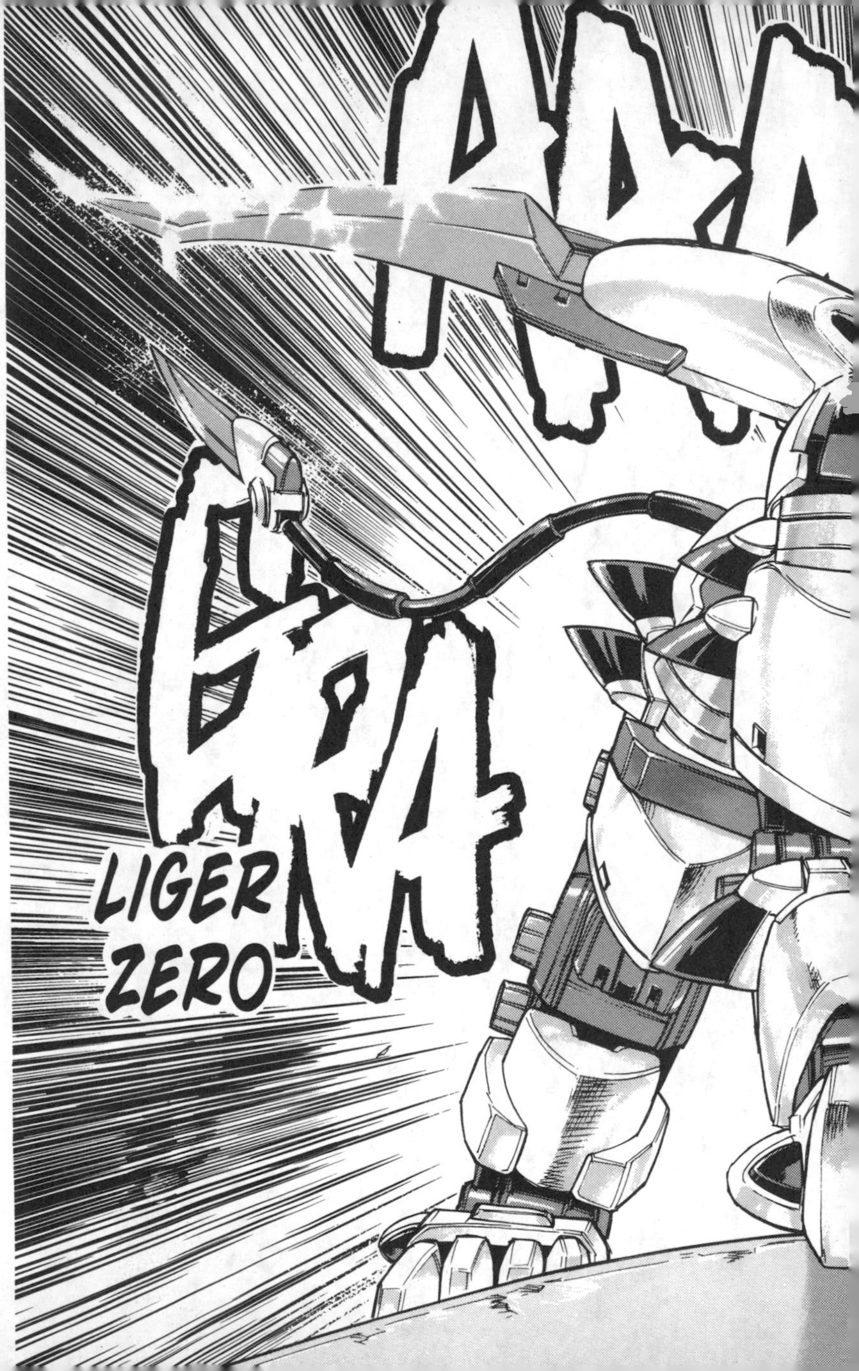
LIGER
ZERO

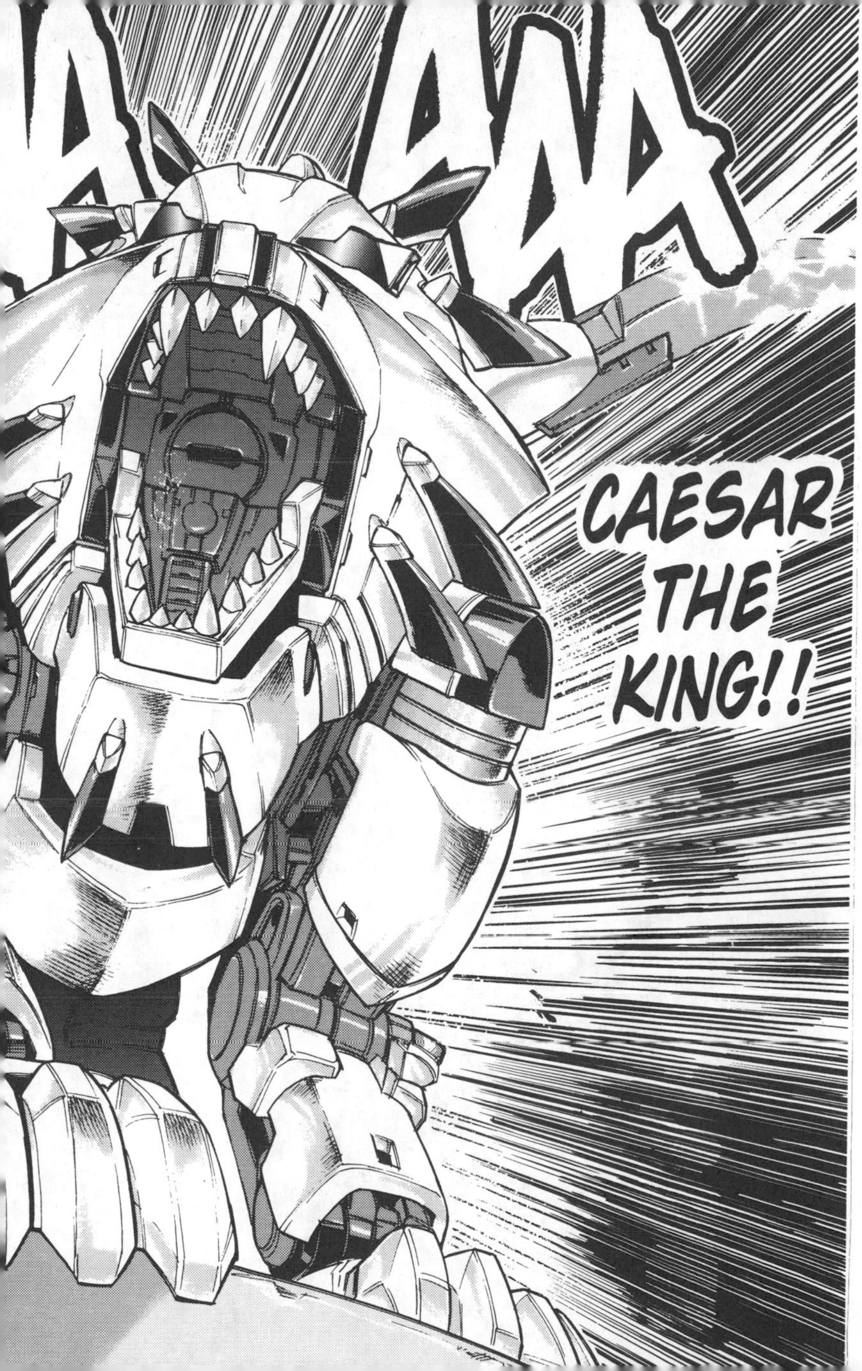
CAESAR THE KING!!

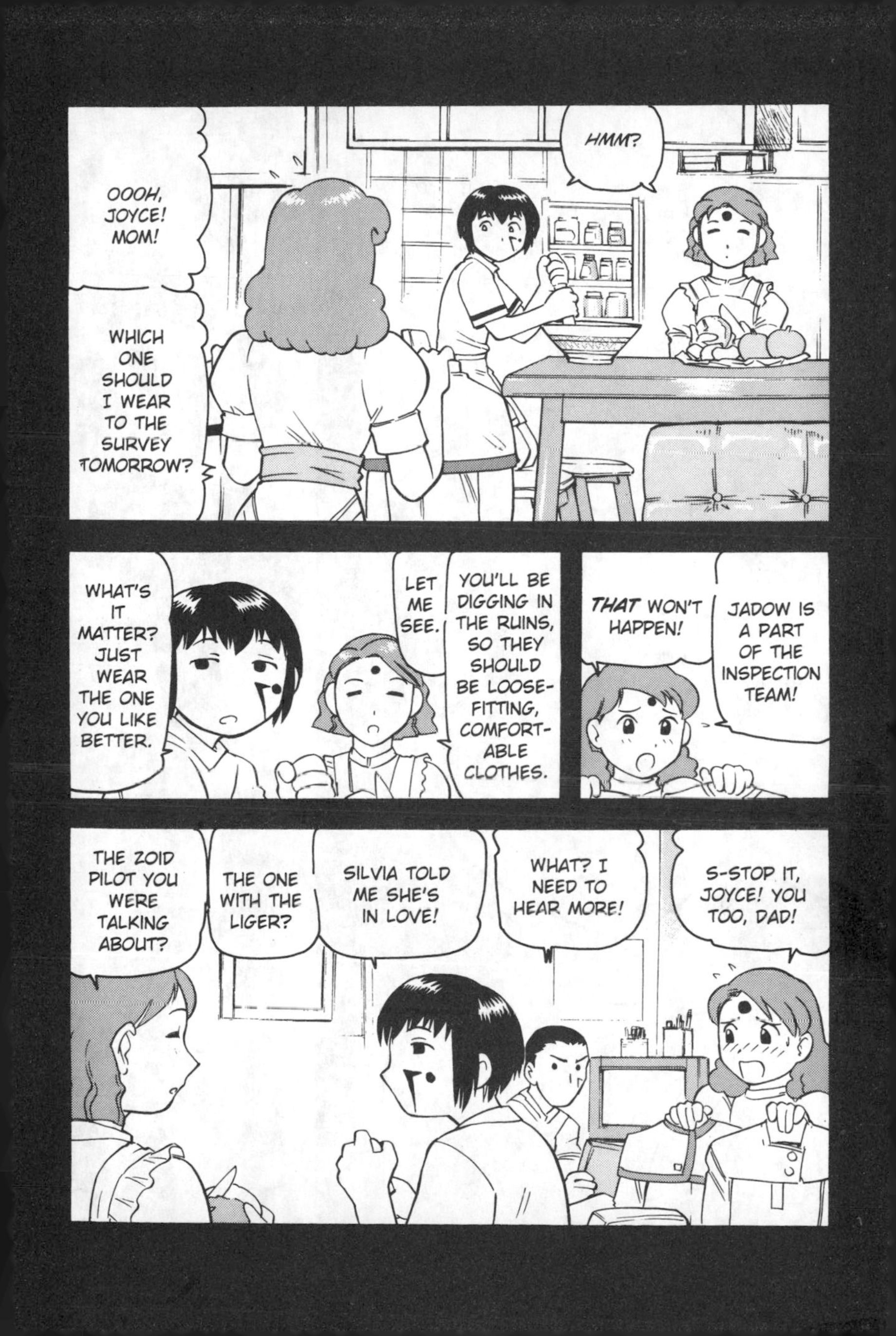
OOOH, JOYCE! MOM!
WHICH ONE SHOULD I WEAR TO THE SURVEY TOMORROW?
HMM?
WHAT'S IT MATTER? JUST WEAR THE ONE YOU LIKE BETTER.
LET ME SEE.
YOU'LL BE DIGGING IN THE RUINS, SO THEY SHOULD BE LOOSE-FITTING, COMFORT-ABLE CLOTHES.
THAT WON'T HAPPEN!
JADOW IS A PART OF THE INSPECTION TEAM!
THE ZOID PILOT YOU WERE TALKING ABOUT?
THE ONE WITH THE LIGER?
SILVIA TOLD ME SHE'S IN LOVE!
WHAT? I NEED TO HEAR MORE!
S-STOP IT, JOYCE! YOU TOO, DAD!

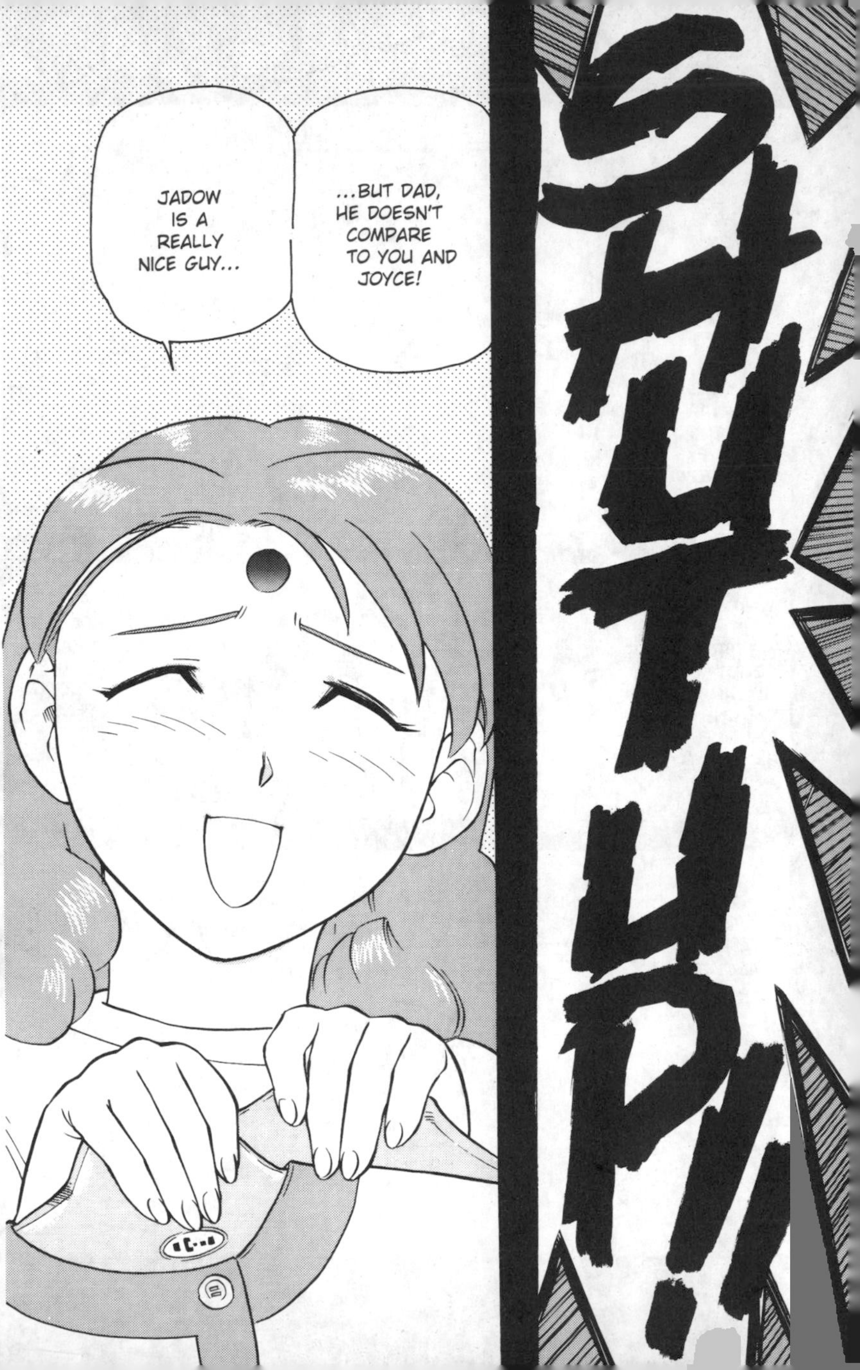
JADOW IS A REALLY NICE GUY...
...BUT DAD, HE DOESN'T COMPARE TO YOU AND JOYCE!

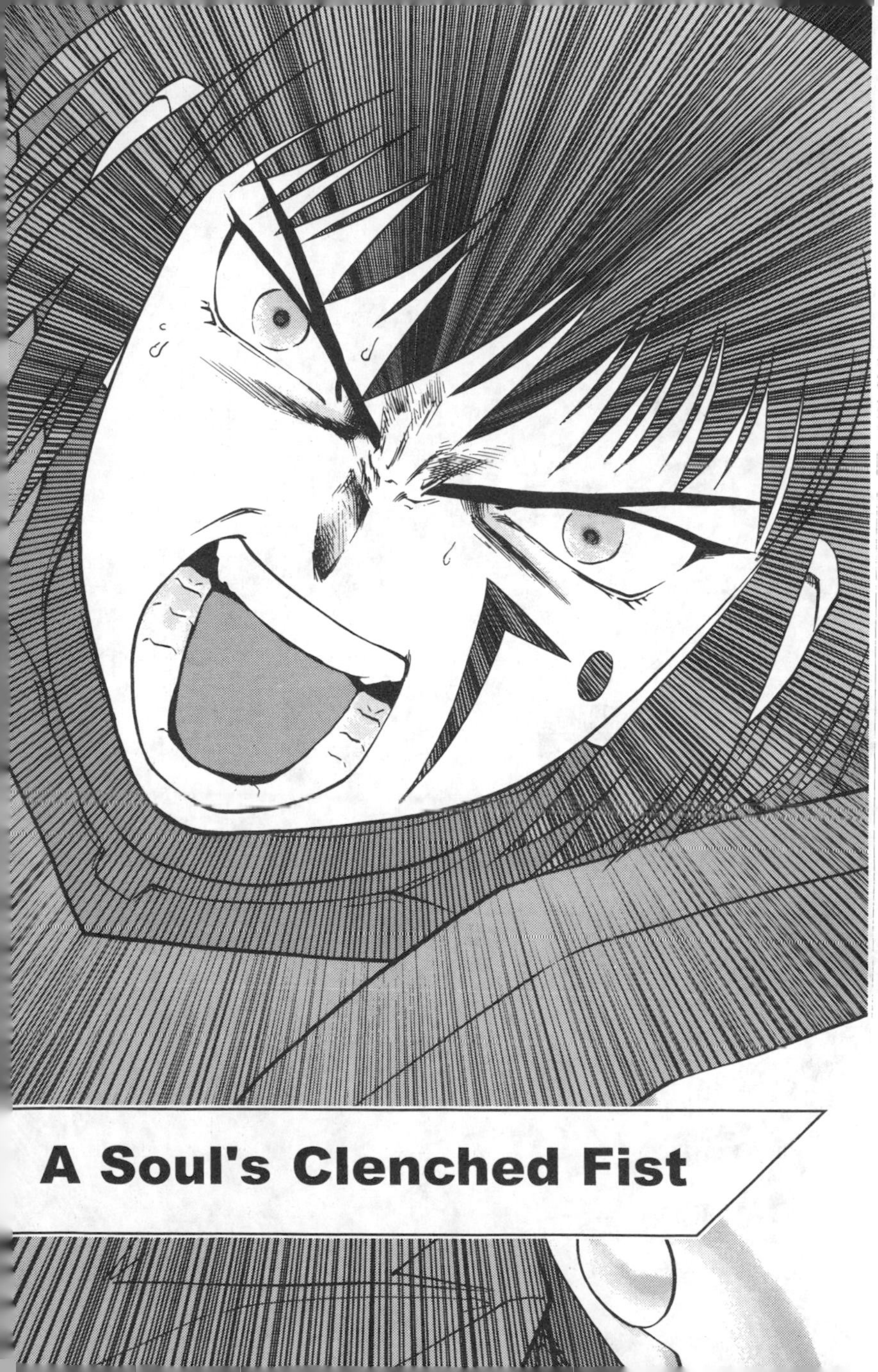
A Soul's Clenched Fist

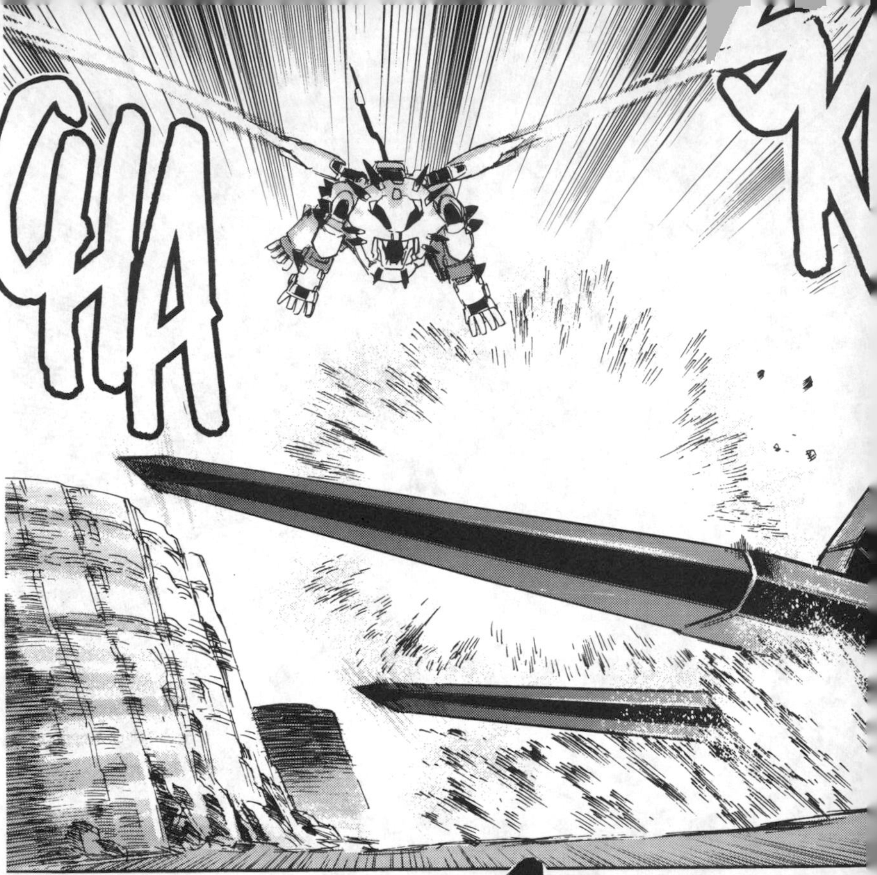
CHAK
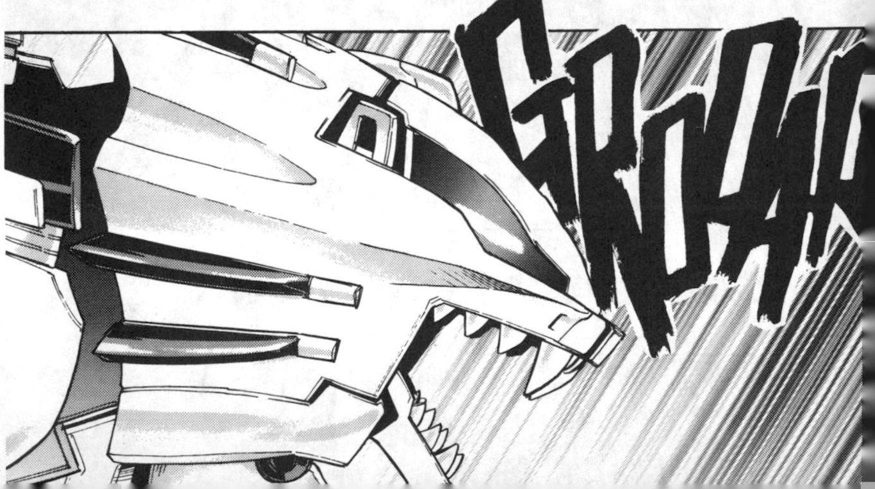
GROAR

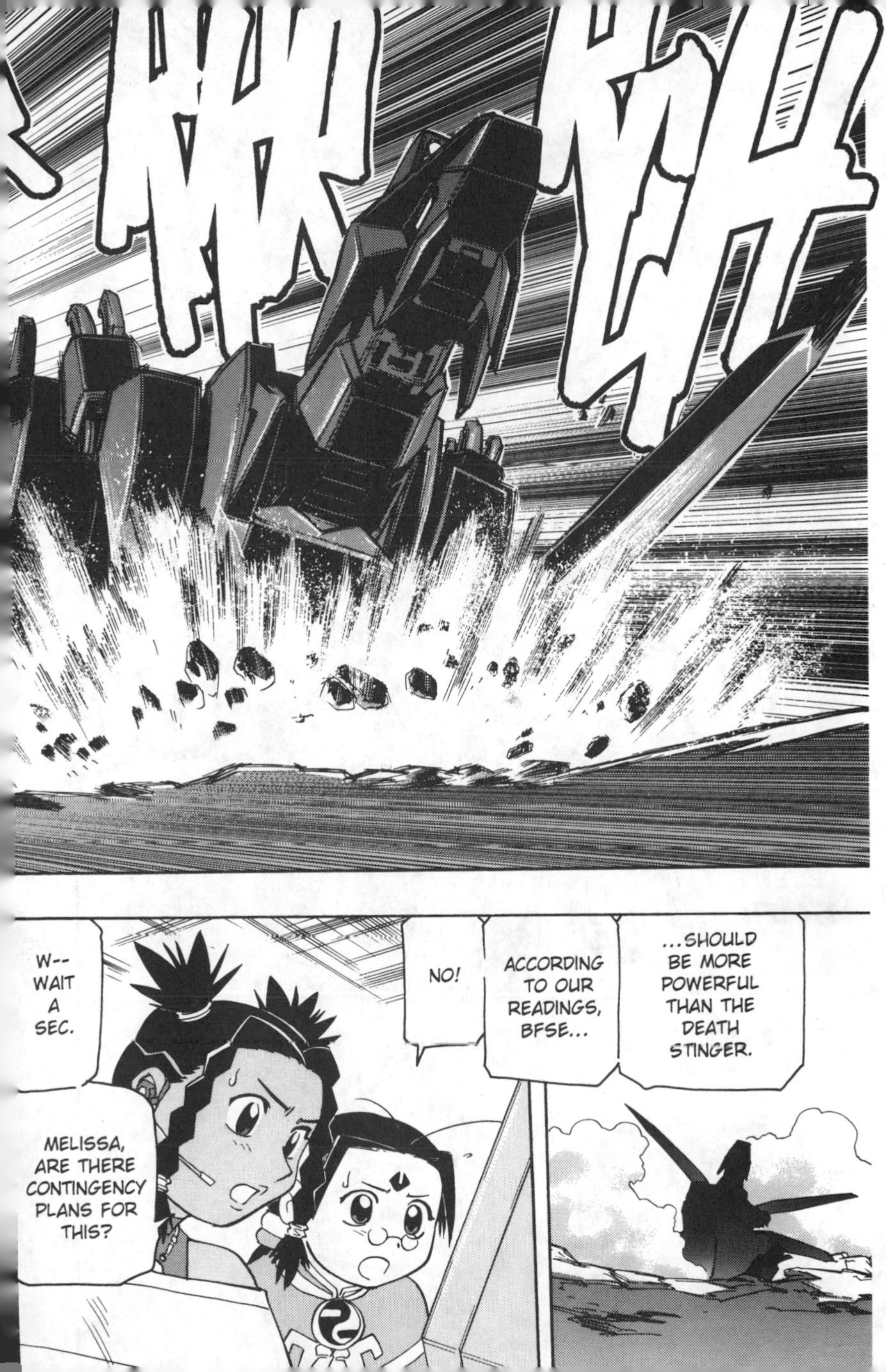
W-- WAIT A SEC.
NO!
ACCORDING TO OUR READINGS, BFSE...
...SHOULD BE MORE POWERFUL THAN THE DEATH STINGER.
MELISSA, ARE THERE CONTINGENCY PLANS FOR THIS?

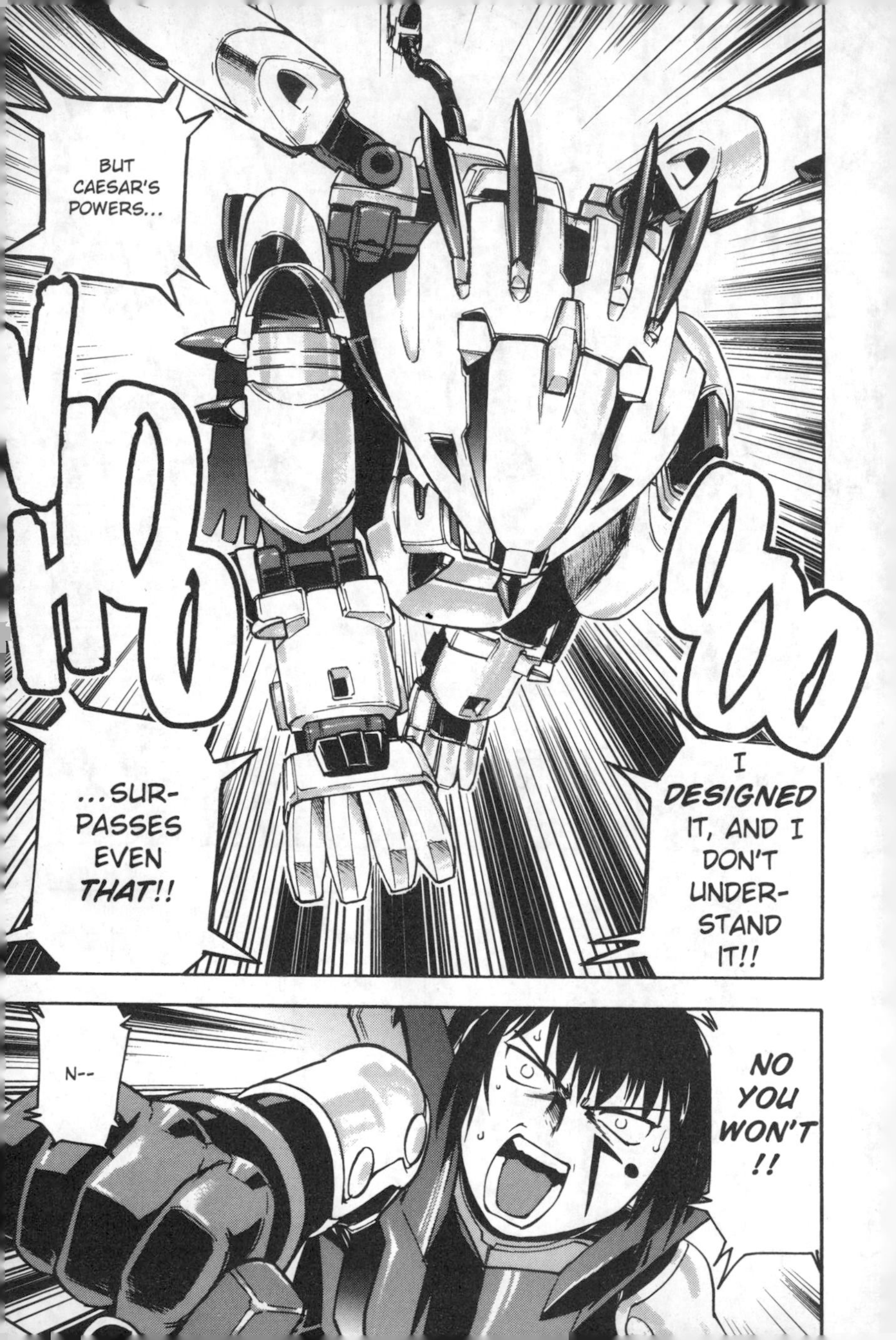
BUT CAESAR'S POWERS...
...SUR-PASSES EVEN THAT!!
I DESIGNED IT, AND I DON'T UNDER-STAND IT!!
N--
NO YOU WON'T !!

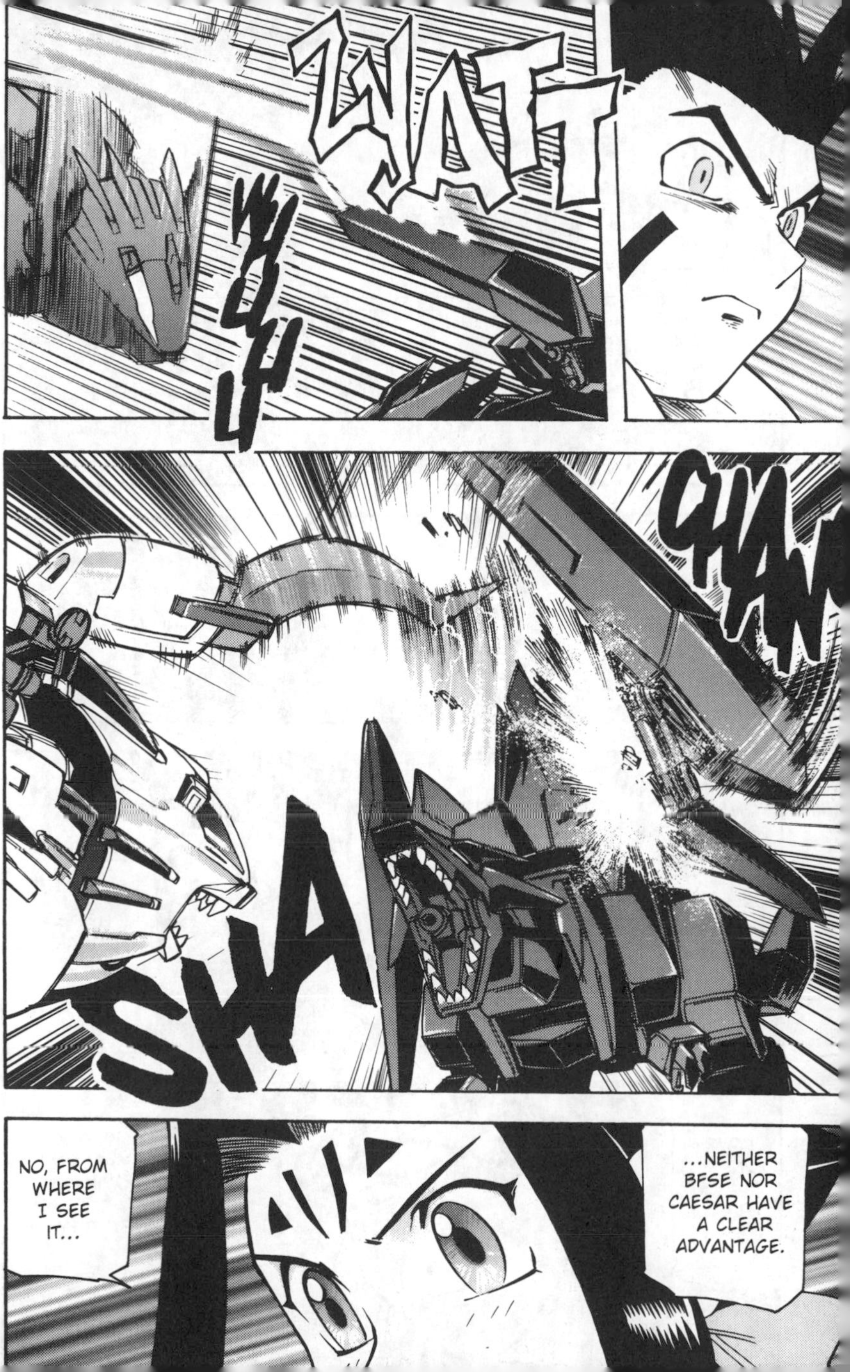
ZWAT
SHA
NO, FROM WHERE I SEE IT...
...NEITHER BFSE NOR CAESAR HAVE A CLEAR ADVANTAGE.

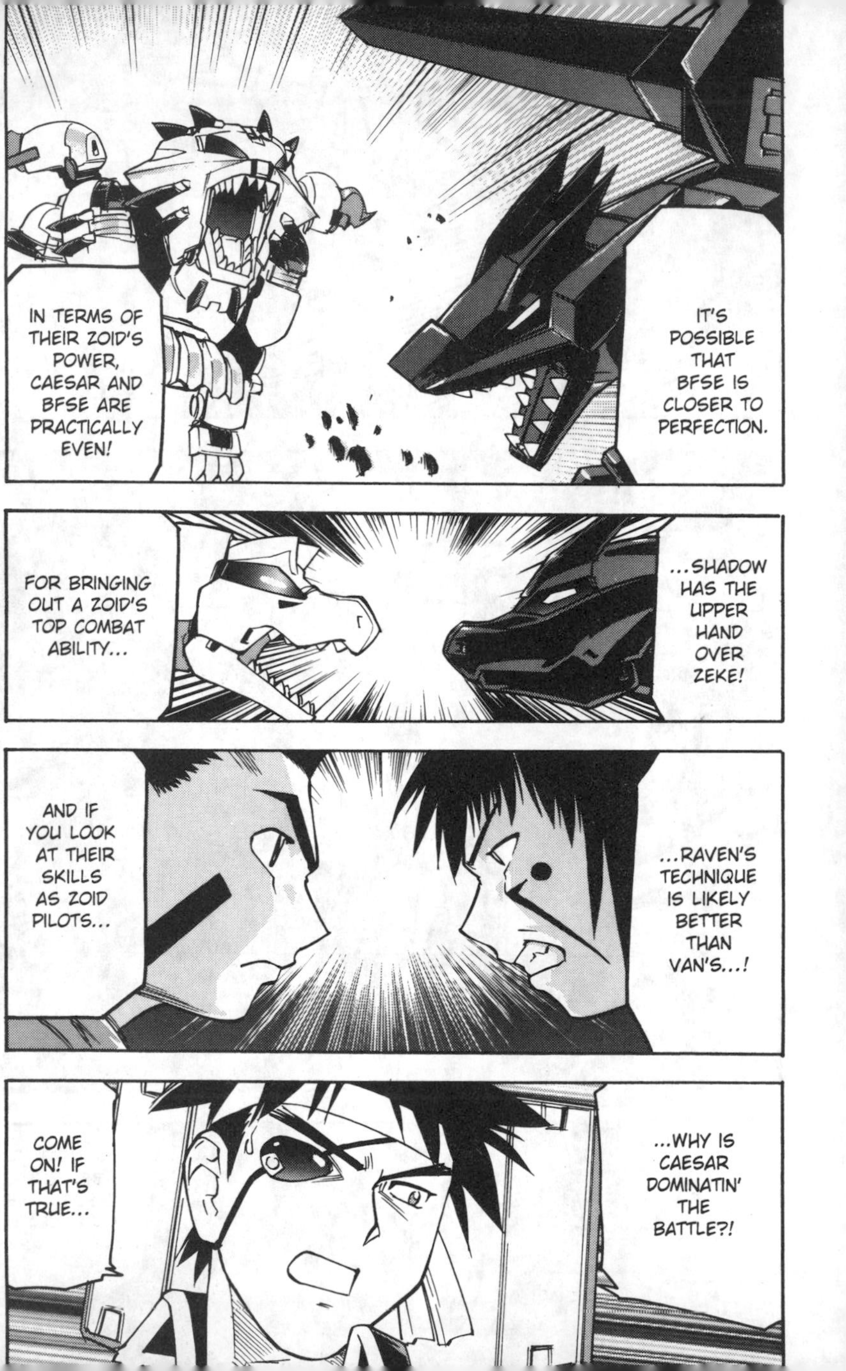
IN TERMS OF THEIR ZOID'S POWER, CAESAR AND BFSE ARE PRACTICALLY EVEN!
IT'S POSSIBLE THAT BFSE IS CLOSER TO PERFECTION.
FOR BRINGING OUT A ZOID'S TOP COMBAT ABILITY...
...SHADOW HAS THE UPPER HAND OVER ZEKE!
AND IF YOU LOOK AT THEIR SKILLS AS ZOID PILOTS...
...RAVEN'S TECHNIQUE IS LIKELY BETTER THAN VAN'S...!
COME ON! IF THAT'S TRUE...
...WHY IS CAESAR DOMINATIN' THE BATTLE?!

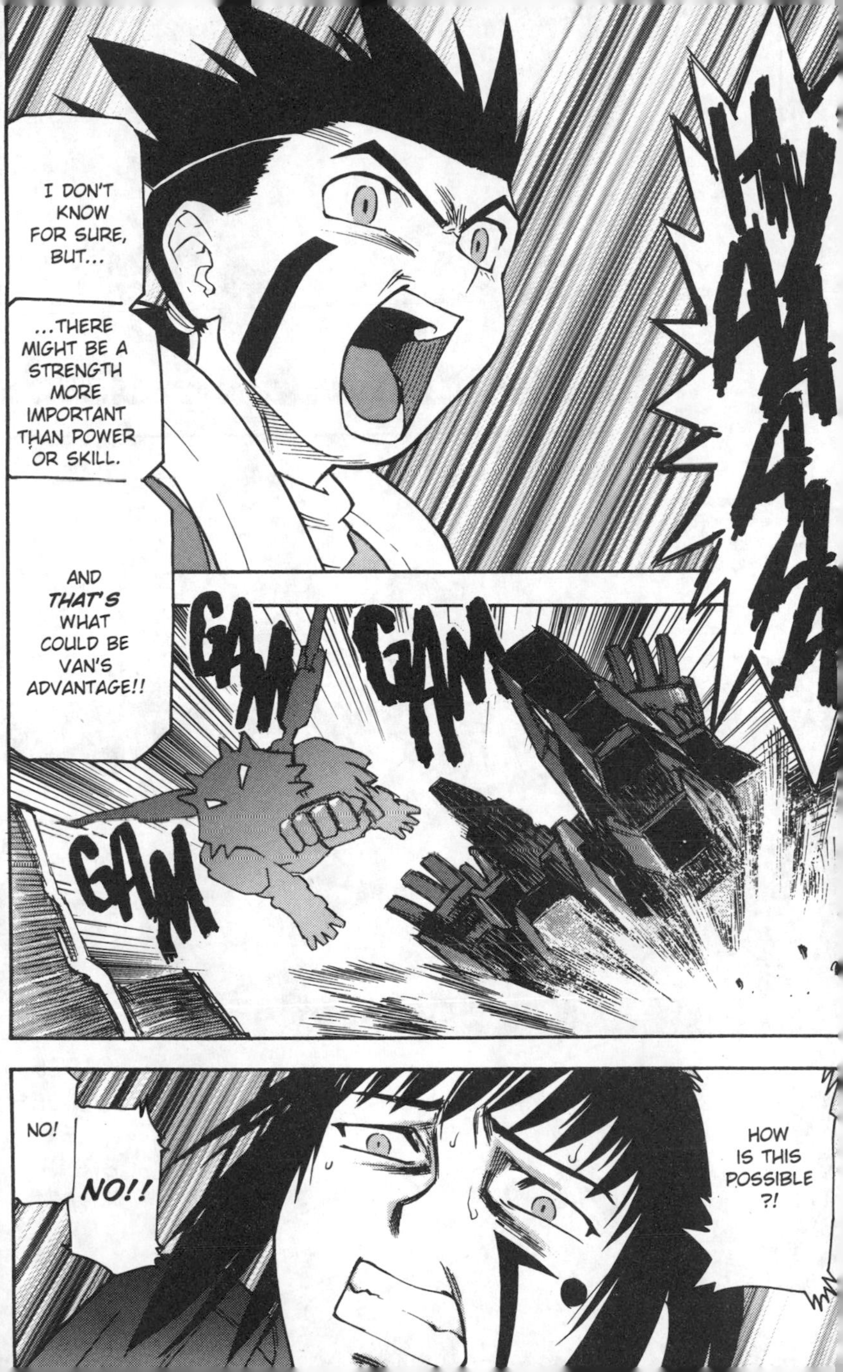
I DON'T KNOW FOR SURE, BUT...
...THERE MIGHT BE A STRENGTH MORE IMPORTANT THAN POWER OR SKILL.
AND *THAT'S* WHAT COULD BE VAN'S ADVANTAGE!!
GAM
GAM
GAM
NO!
NO!!
HOW IS THIS POSSIBLE ?!

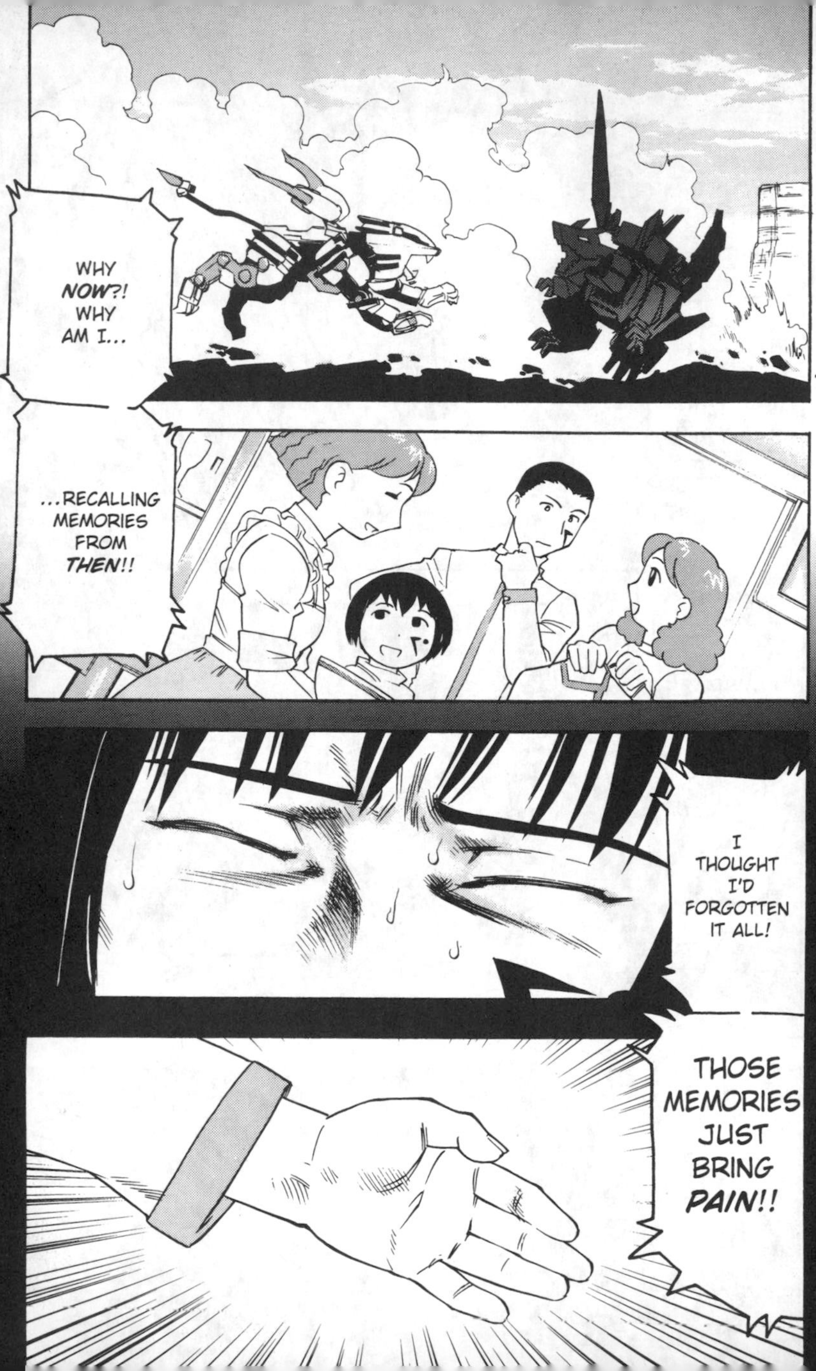
WHY *NOW?!* WHY AM I...
...RECALLING MEMORIES FROM *THEN!!*
I THOUGHT I'D FORGOTTEN IT ALL!
THOSE MEMORIES JUST BRING *PAIN!!*

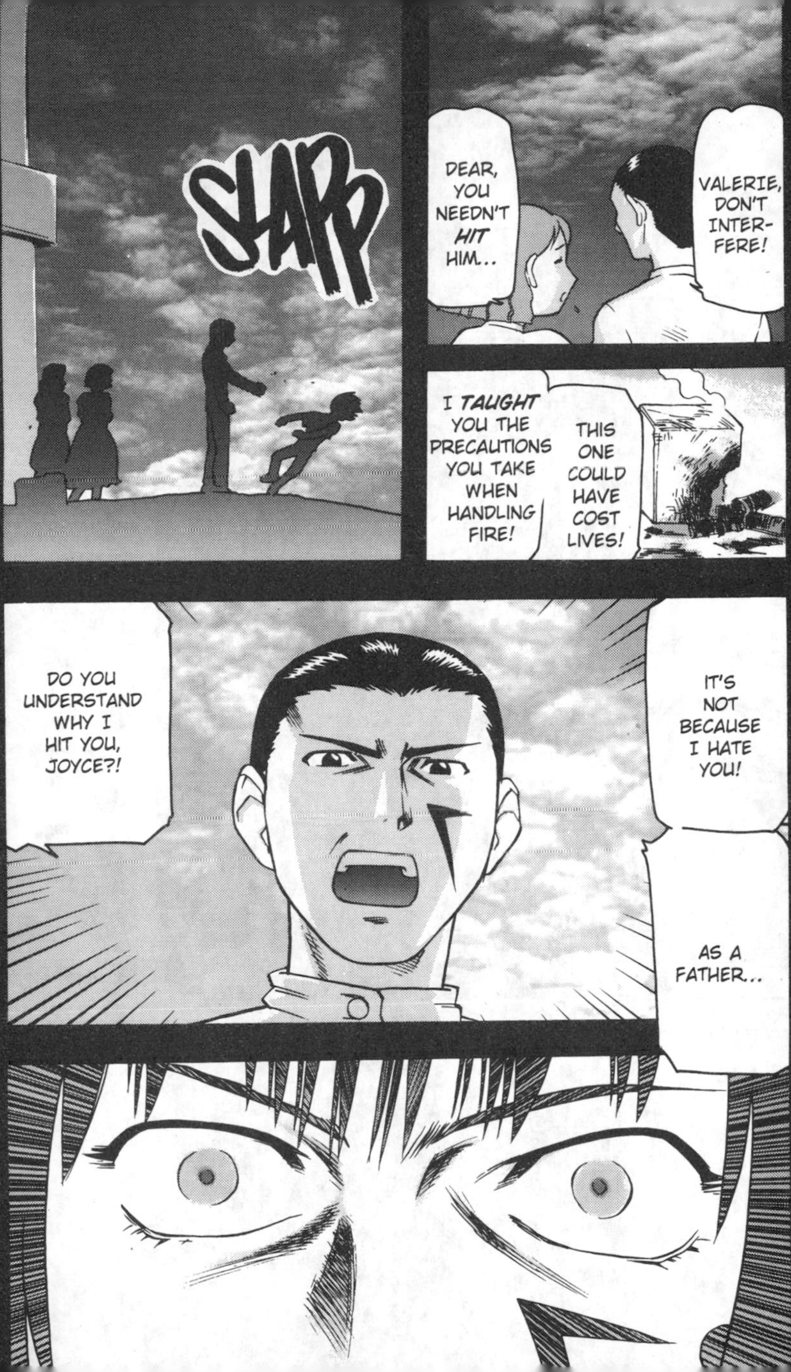
SLAP
DEAR, YOU NEEDN'T *HIT* HIM...
VALERIE, DON'T INTER-FERE!
I *TAUGHT* YOU THE PRECAUTIONS YOU TAKE WHEN HANDLING FIRE!
THIS ONE COULD HAVE COST LIVES!
DO YOU UNDERSTAND WHY I HIT YOU, JOYCE?!
IT'S NOT BECAUSE I HATE YOU!
AS A FATHER...

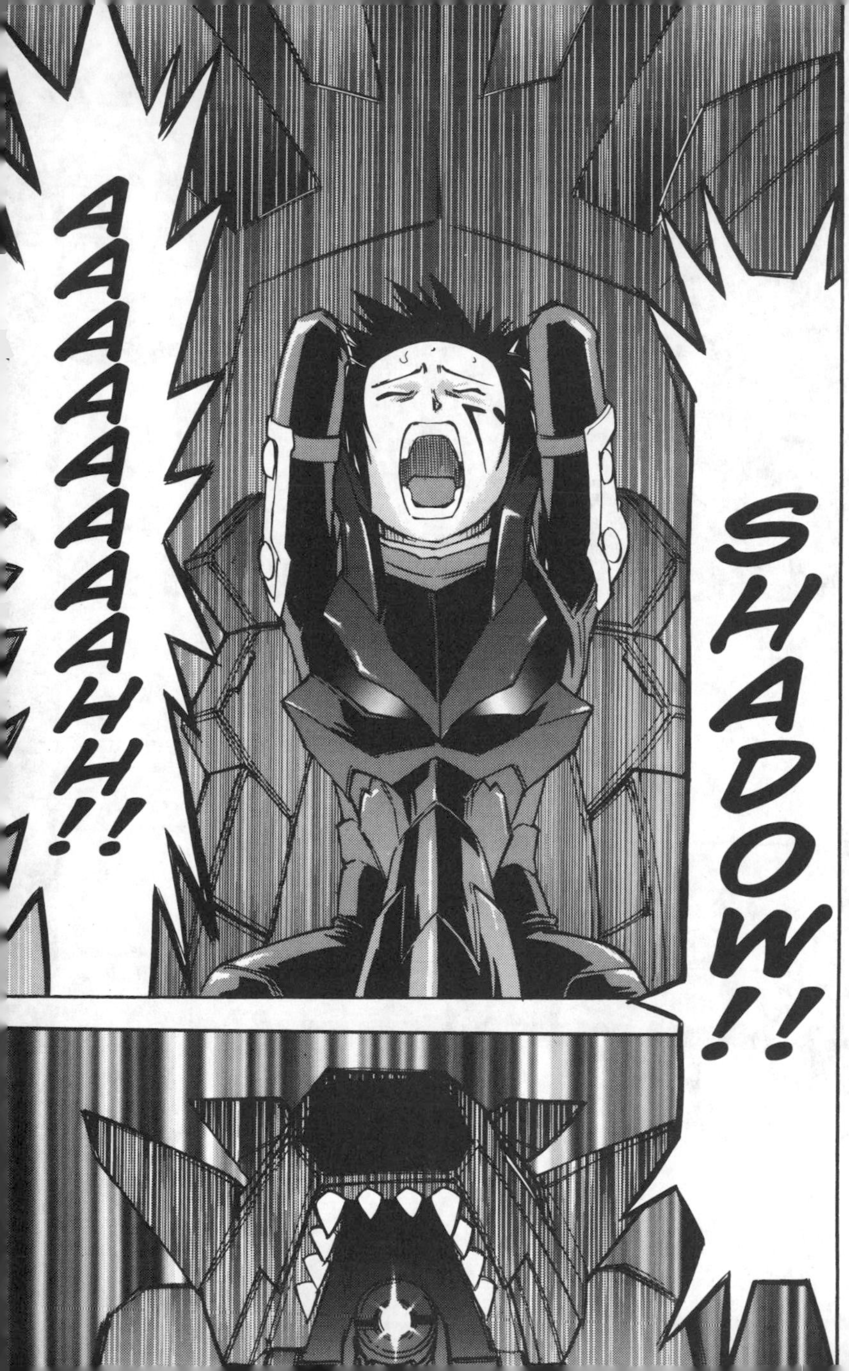
SHADOW!!
AAAAAAAAHH!!

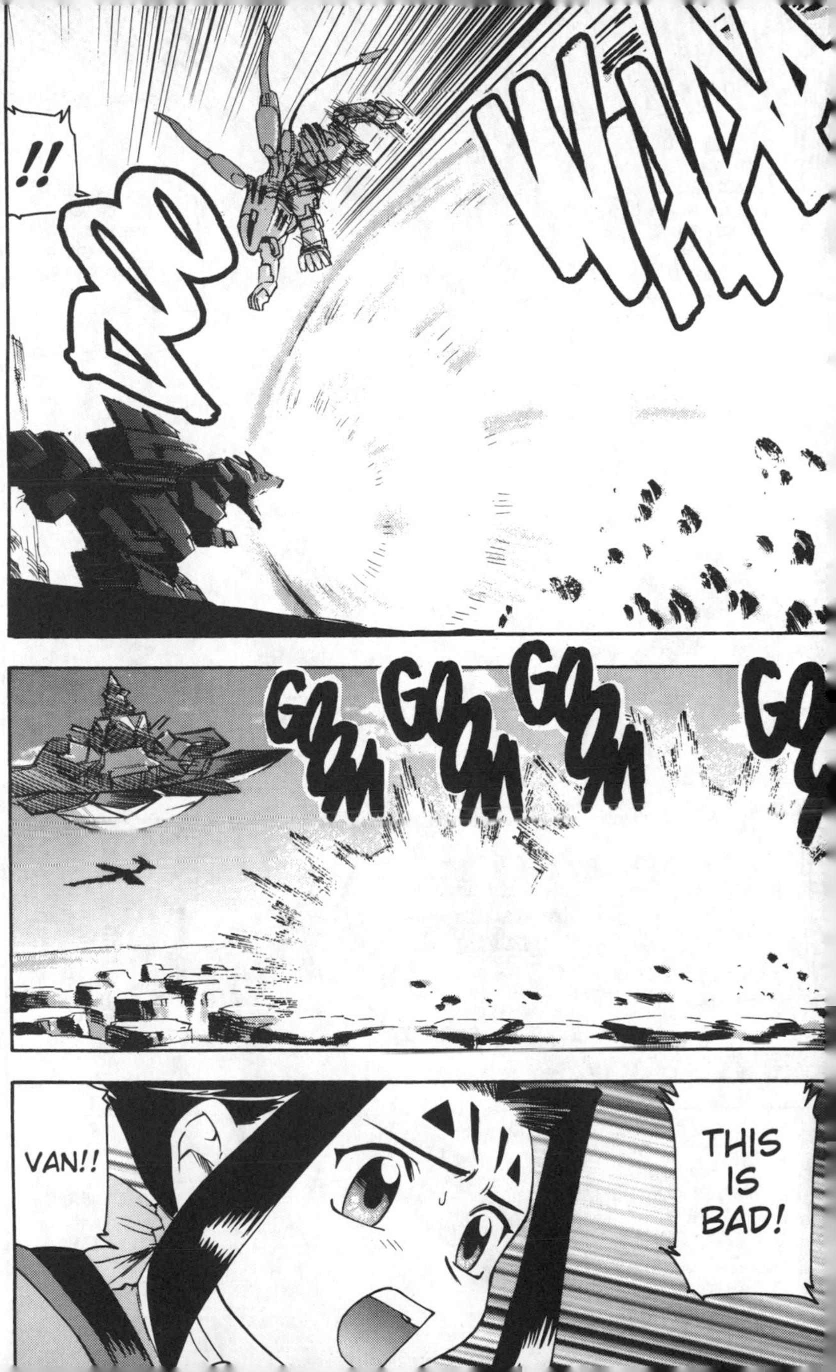
!!
DO
WHAM
GOOM GOOM GOOM GO
VAN!!
THIS IS BAD!

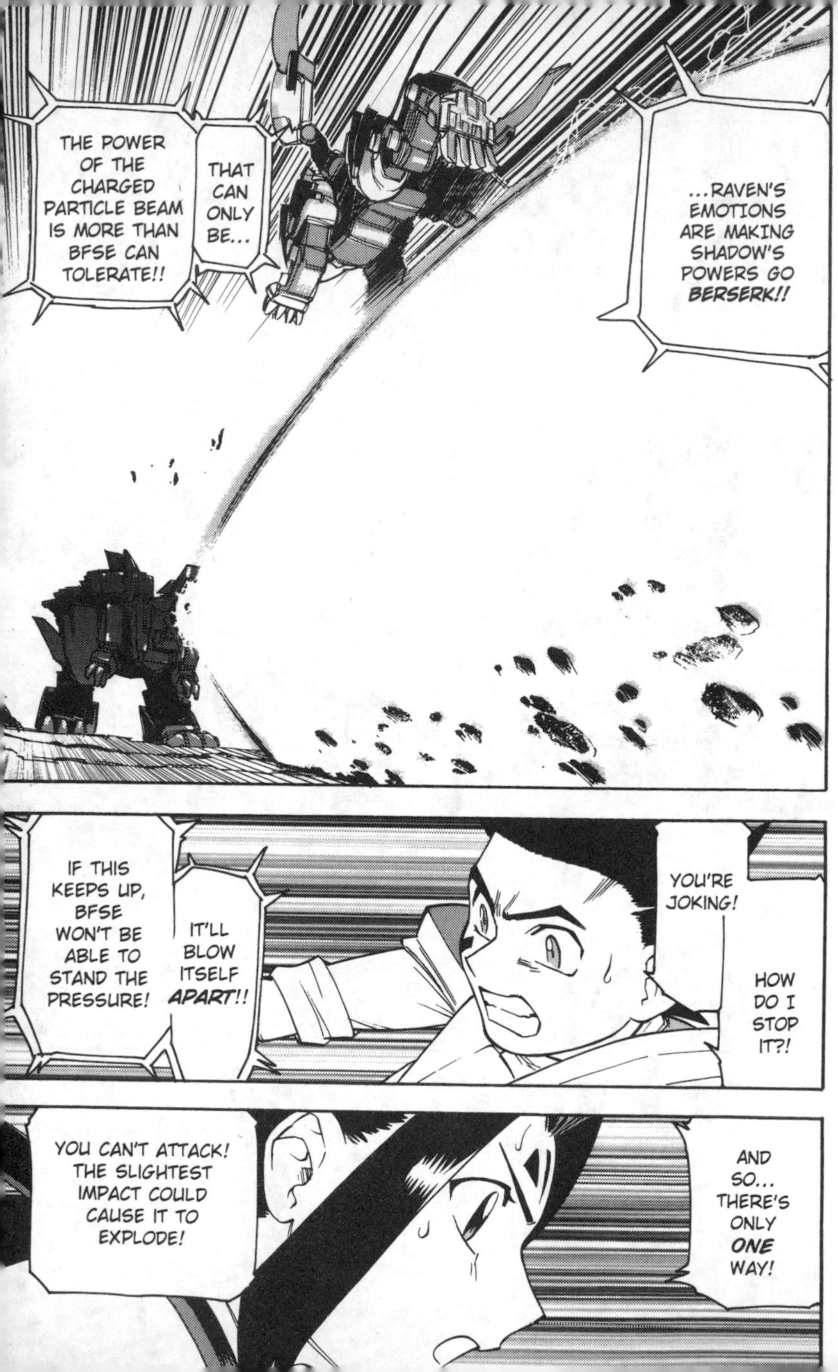
THE POWER OF THE CHARGED PARTICLE BEAM IS MORE THAN BFSE CAN TOLERATE!!
THAT CAN ONLY BE...
...RAVEN'S EMOTIONS ARE MAKING SHADOW'S POWERS GO BERSERK!!
IF THIS KEEPS UP, BFSE WON'T BE ABLE TO STAND THE PRESSURE!
IT'LL BLOW ITSELF APART!!
YOU'RE JOKING!
HOW DO I STOP IT?!
YOU CAN'T ATTACK! THE SLIGHTEST IMPACT COULD CAUSE IT TO EXPLODE!
AND SO... THERE'S ONLY ONE WAY!

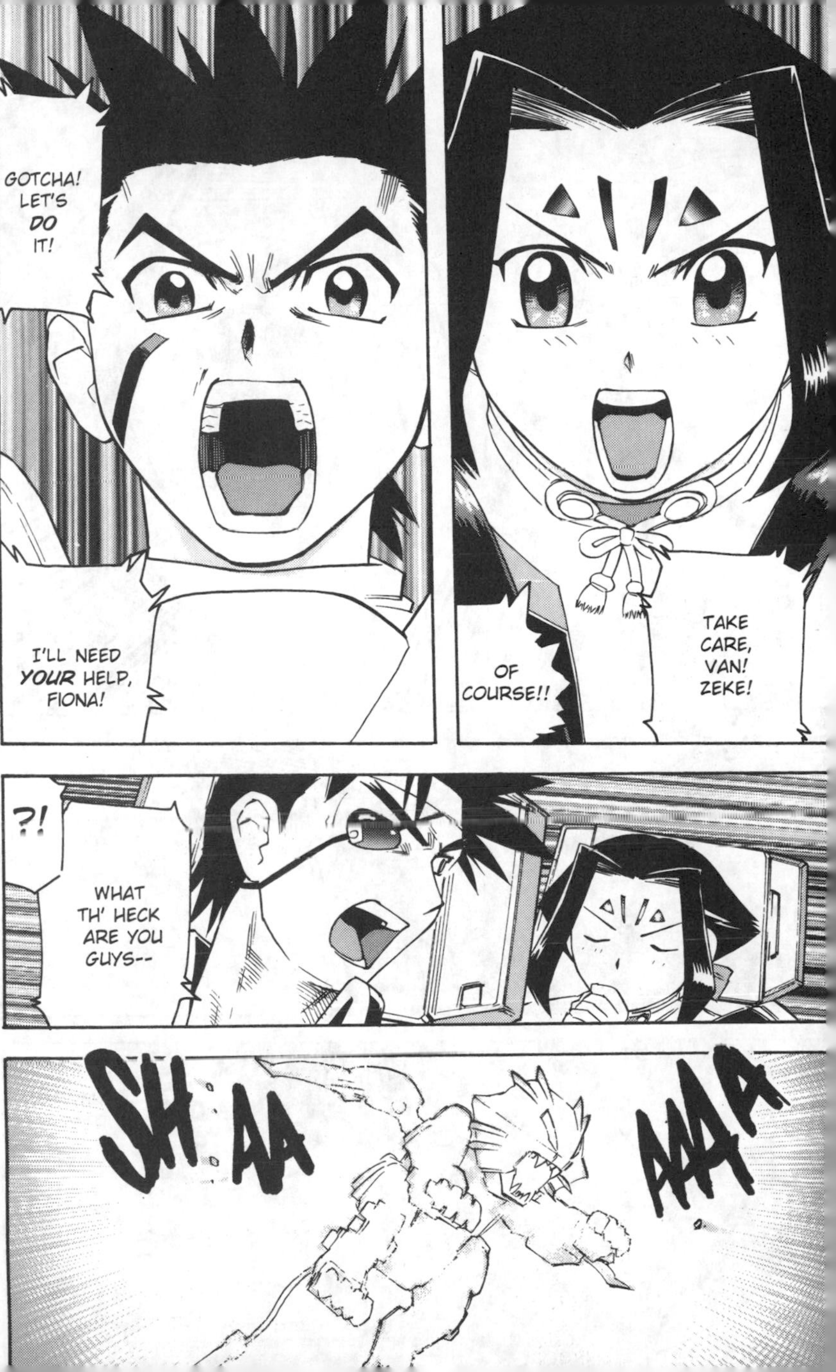
GOTCHA! LET'S ***DO*** IT!
I'LL NEED ***YOUR*** HELP, FIONA!
OF COURSE!!
TAKE CARE, VAN! ZEKE!
?!
WHAT TH' HECK ARE YOU GUYS--
SHAA AAAA

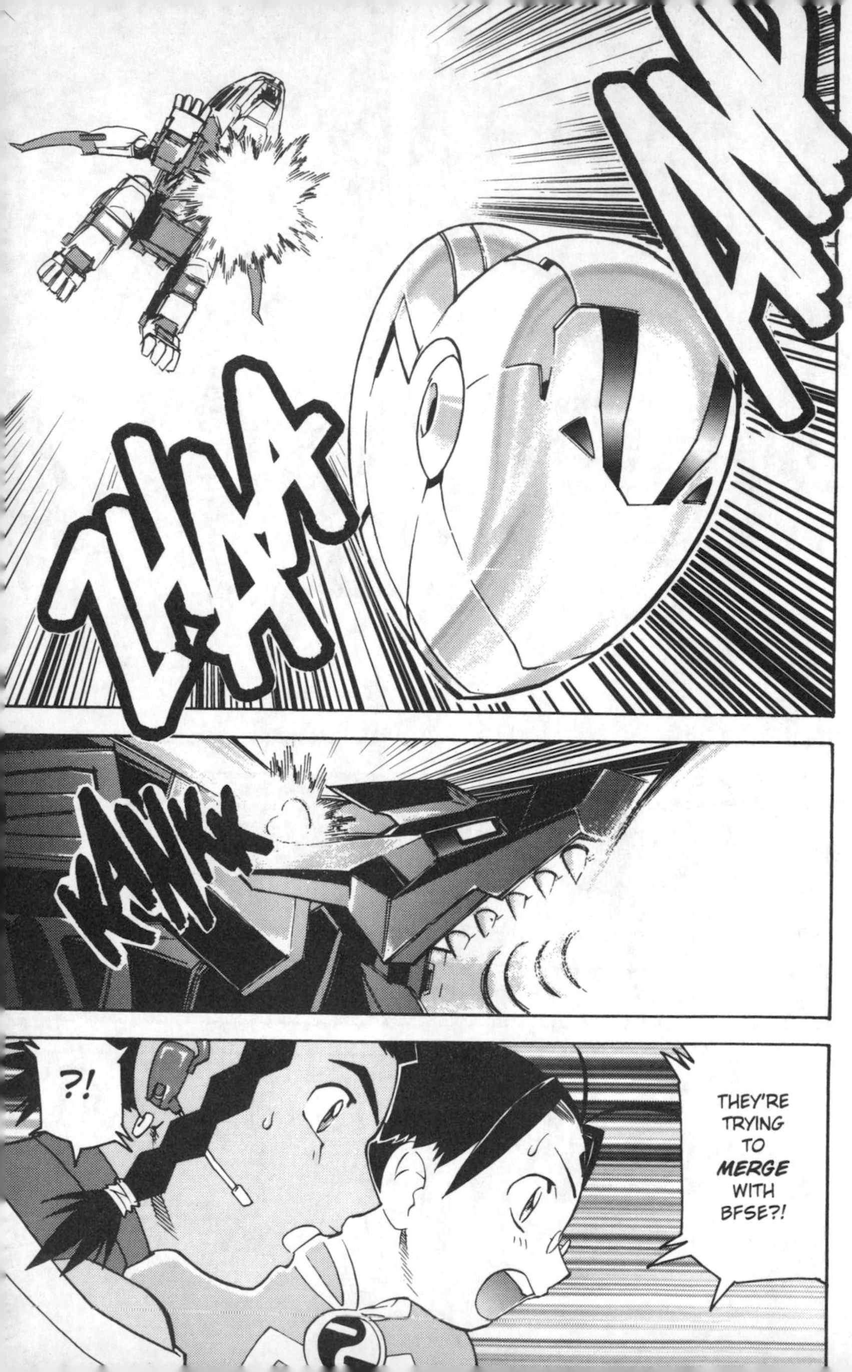
?!
THEY'RE TRYING TO *MERGE* WITH BFSE?!

GOOM GOOM GOOM GOOM GOOM GOOM

B-BUT BFSE IS *ALREADY* MERGED WITH SHADOW!

AND MORE IMPORTANT... ZEKE CAN'T MERGE UNLESS THE ZOID OPENS ITS HEART!!

NO... THIS TIME THEY *CAN!*

THERE WAS A TIME BEFORE WHEN THEY DID!

AND THAT TIME, THE KEY WAS...

FIONA!!!

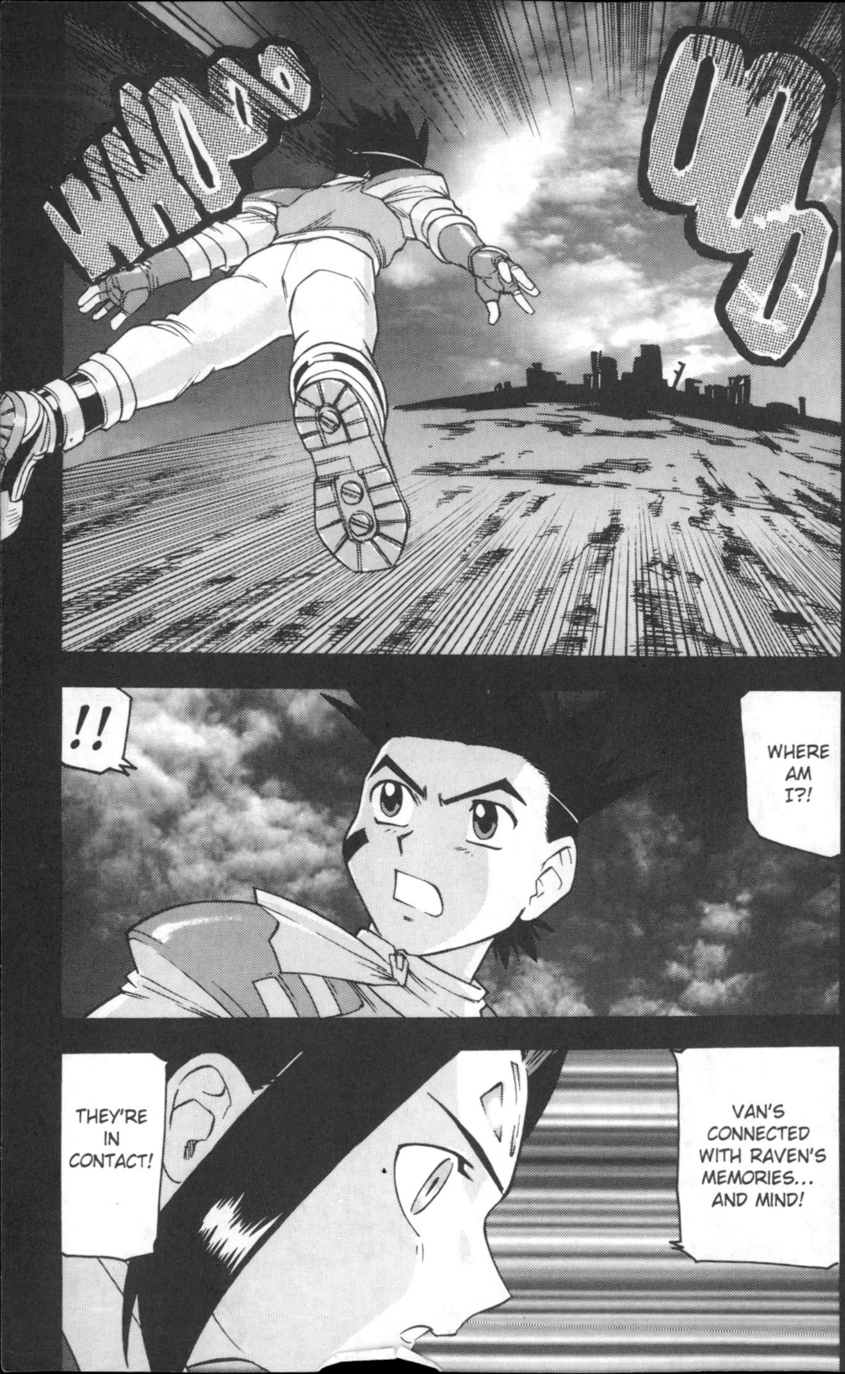
WHOA!
OOF!
!!
WHERE AM I?!
THEY'RE IN CONTACT!
VAN'S CONNECTED WITH RAVEN'S MEMORIES... AND MIND!

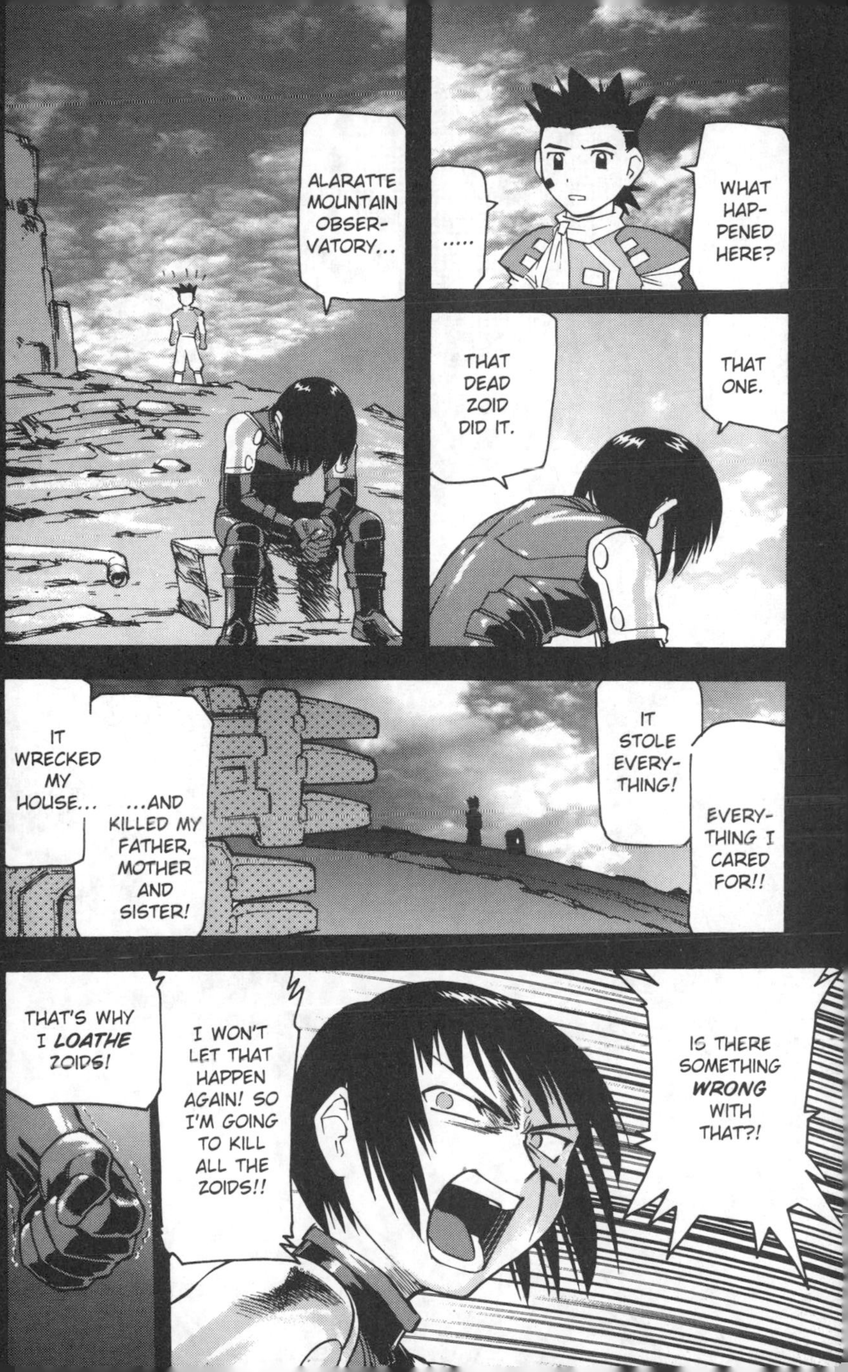
ALARATTE MOUNTAIN OBSERVATORY...
.....
WHAT HAPPENED HERE?
THAT DEAD ZOID DID IT.
THAT ONE.
IT WRECKED MY HOUSE...
...AND KILLED MY FATHER, MOTHER AND SISTER!
IT STOLE EVERYTHING!
EVERYTHING I CARED FOR!!
THAT'S WHY I *LOATHE* ZOIDS!
I WON'T LET THAT HAPPEN AGAIN! SO I'M GOING TO KILL ALL THE ZOIDS!!
IS THERE SOMETHING **WRONG** WITH THAT?!

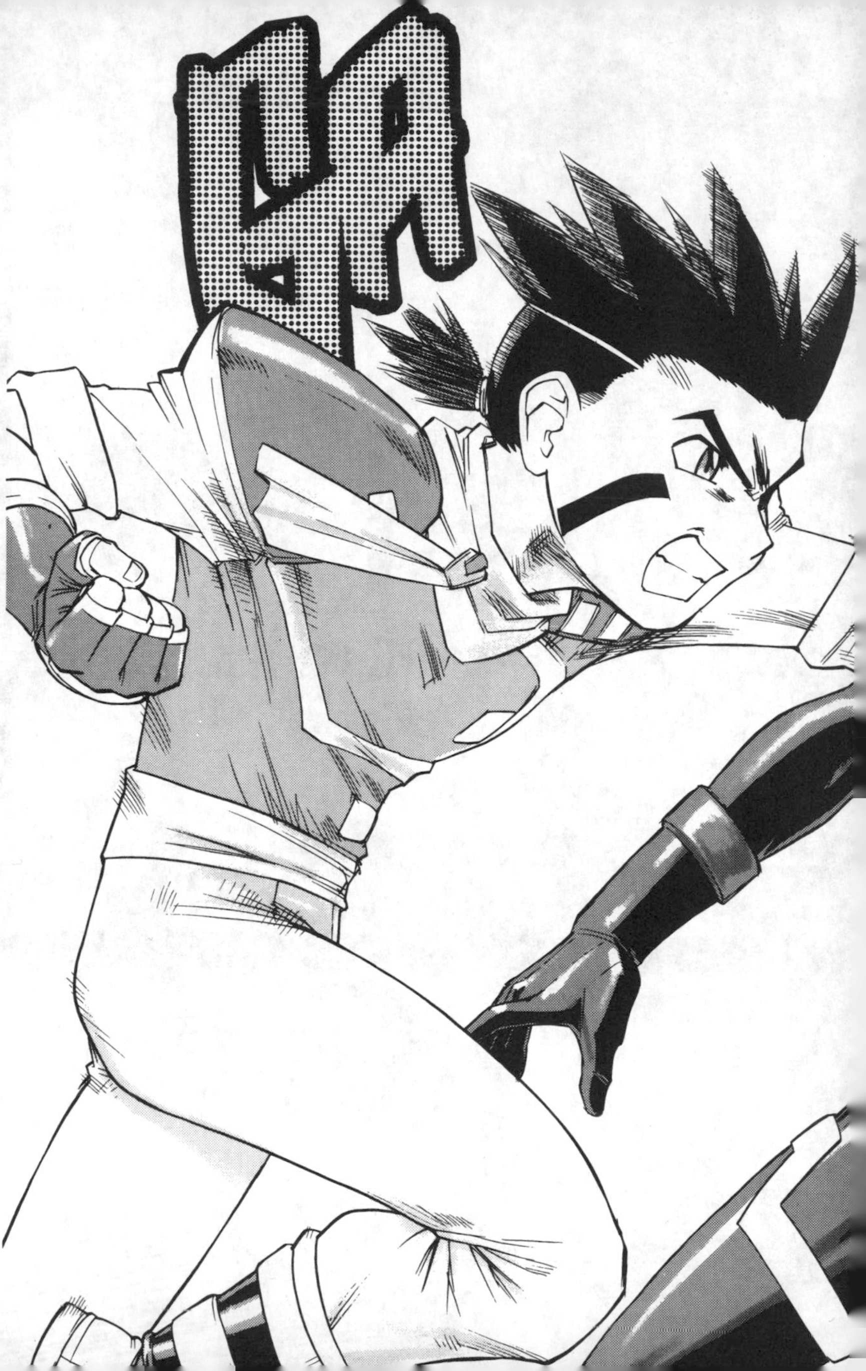

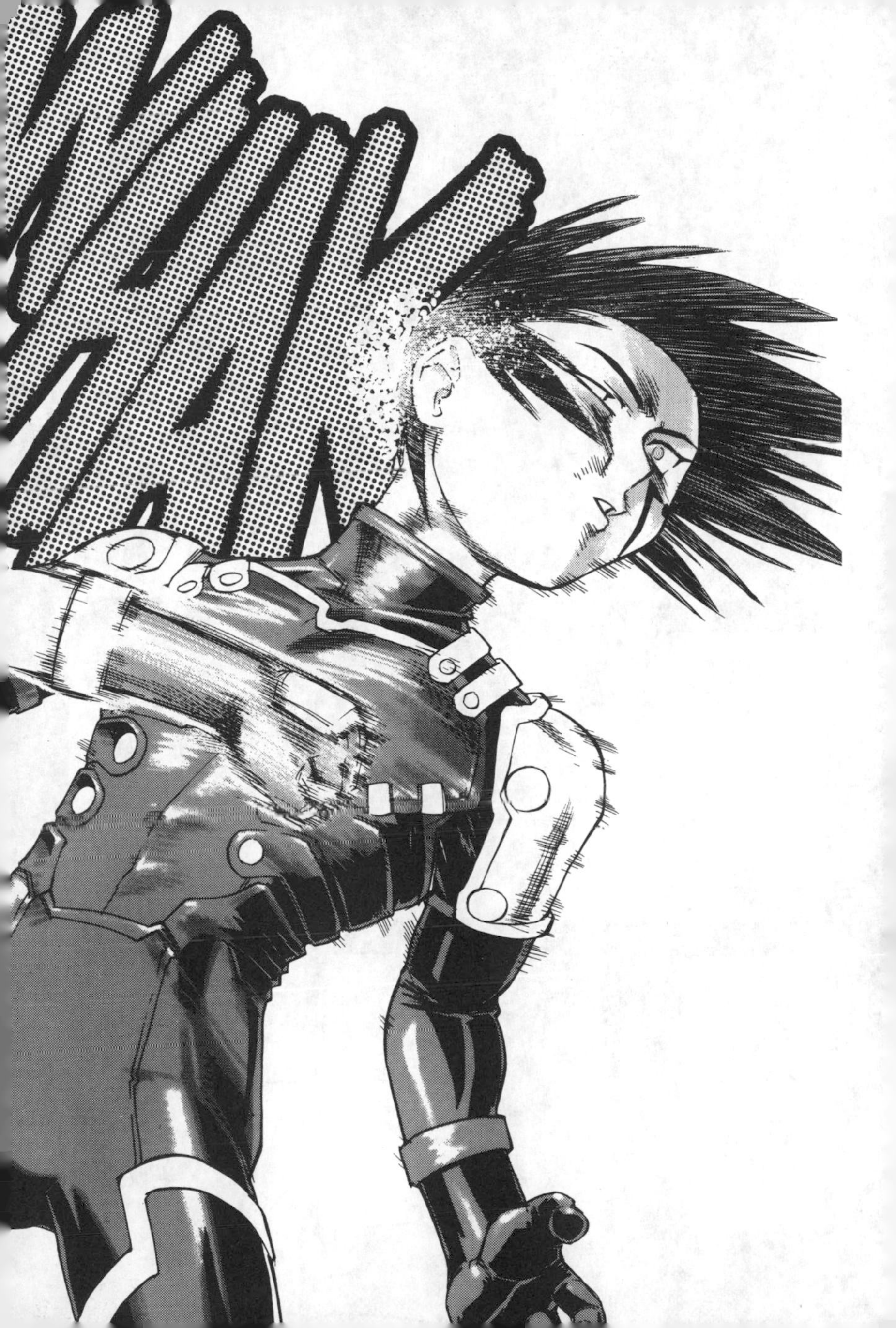

.....
!!

KOMBA!

KLATTA
KLATTA

IT *IS*
WRONG!

AND YOU
KNOW
IT!!

DONNIE
AND HIS
FAMILY
DID A
THOROUGH
INVESTIGATION
ON THIS
SITE!

THE
RESULTS
...

...TOLD THEM THAT
THE ZOID WAS
INFECTED BY A
VIRUS THAT
DISABLED ITS
BRAIN FUNCTION!

THE ZOID
WENT OUT
OF CONTROL!
BUT IT
WASN'T
THE ZOID'S
FAULT!!

IT
WAS A
TRAGEDY,
BUT IT
WAS AN
ACCIDENT!!

AN
ACCI-
DENT?!

THAT'S
IT?

GRMP

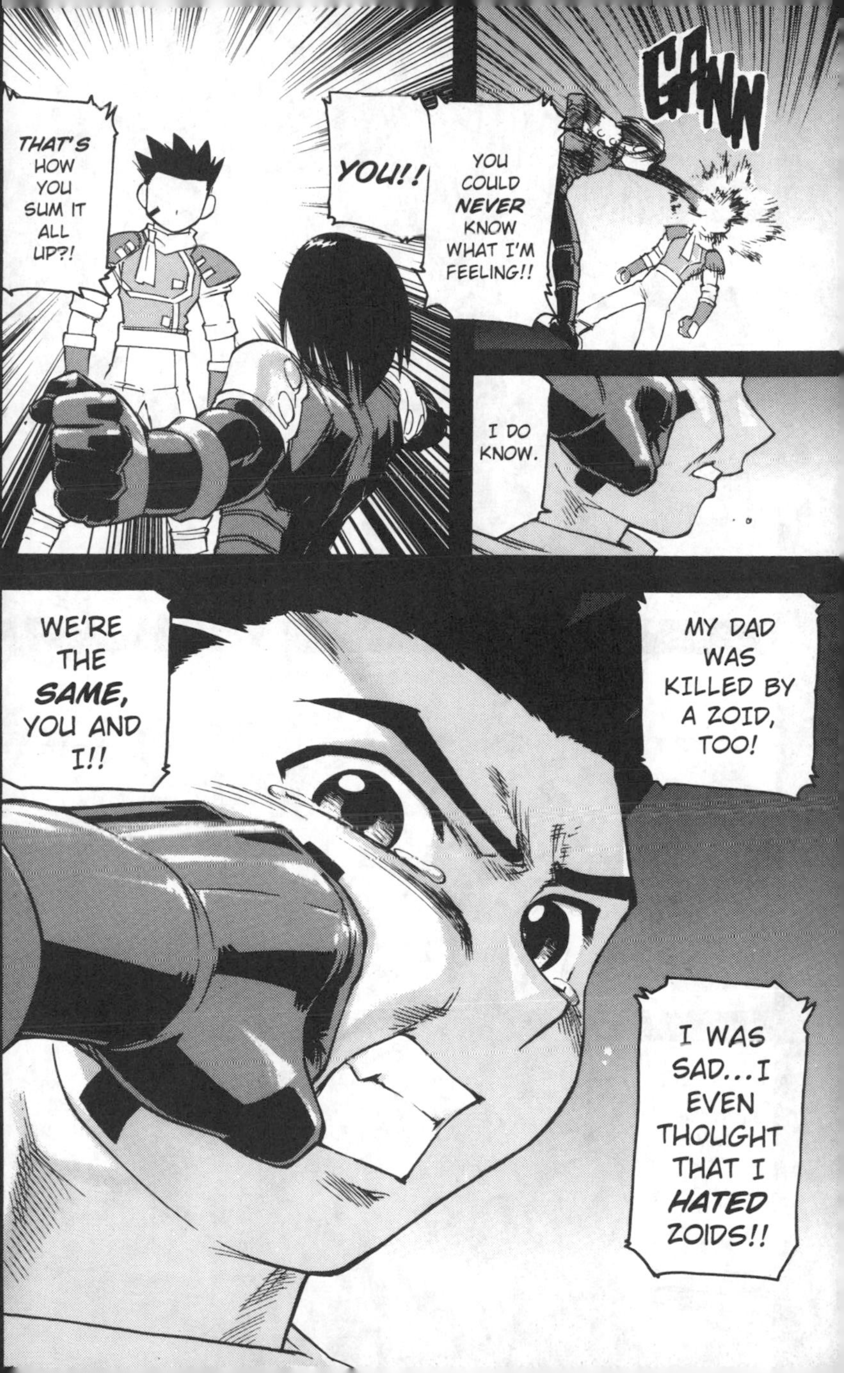
THAT'S HOW YOU SUM IT ALL UP?!
YOU!!
YOU COULD NEVER KNOW WHAT I'M FEELING!!
GAANN
I DO KNOW.
WE'RE THE SAME, YOU AND I!!
MY DAD WAS KILLED BY A ZOID, TOO!
I WAS SAD...I EVEN THOUGHT THAT I HATED ZOIDS!!

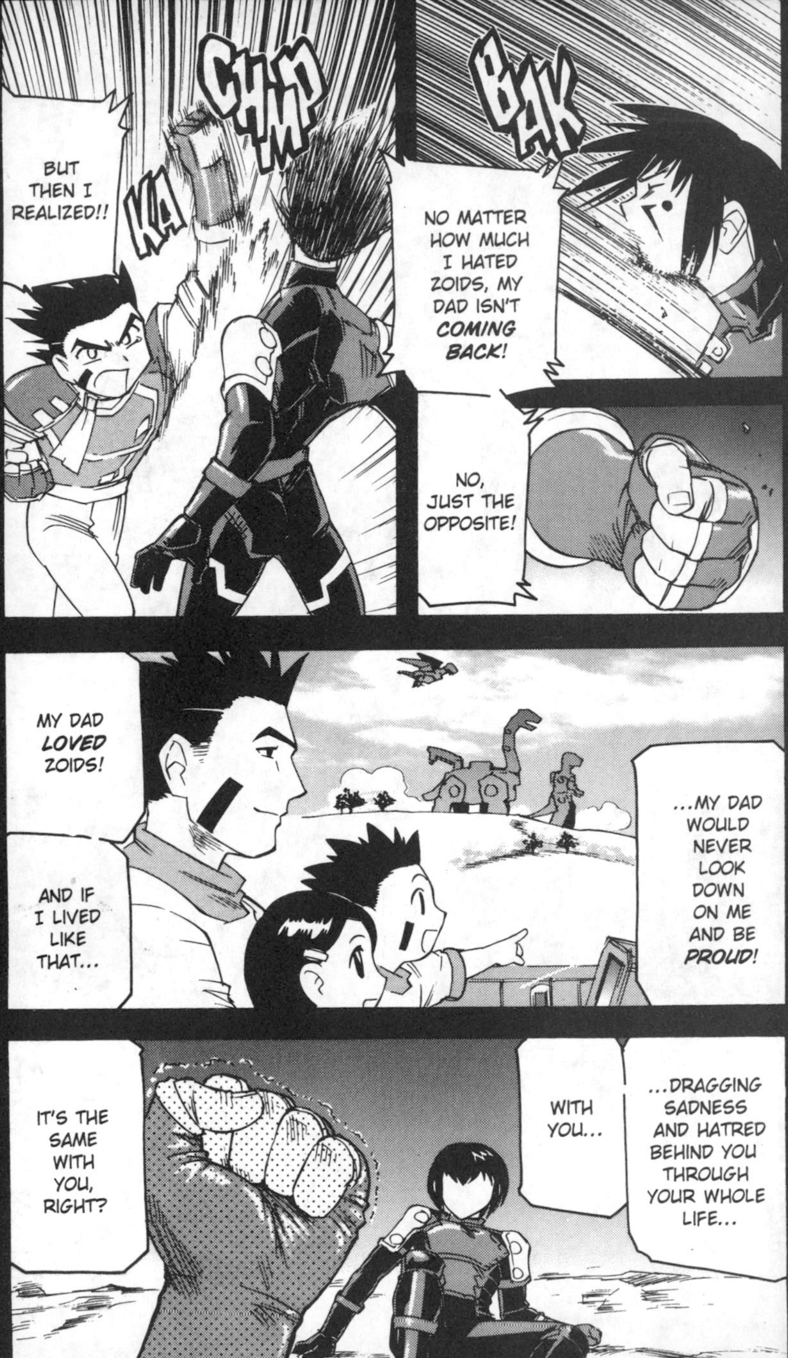
CHOMP
KA
BUT THEN I REALIZED!!
BAK
NO MATTER HOW MUCH I HATED ZOIDS, MY DAD ISN'T *COMING BACK!*
NO, JUST THE OPPOSITE!
MY DAD *LOVED* ZOIDS!
AND IF I LIVED LIKE THAT...
...MY DAD WOULD NEVER LOOK DOWN ON ME AND BE *PROUD!*
IT'S THE SAME WITH YOU, RIGHT?
WITH YOU...
...DRAGGING SADNESS AND HATRED BEHIND YOU THROUGH YOUR WHOLE LIFE...

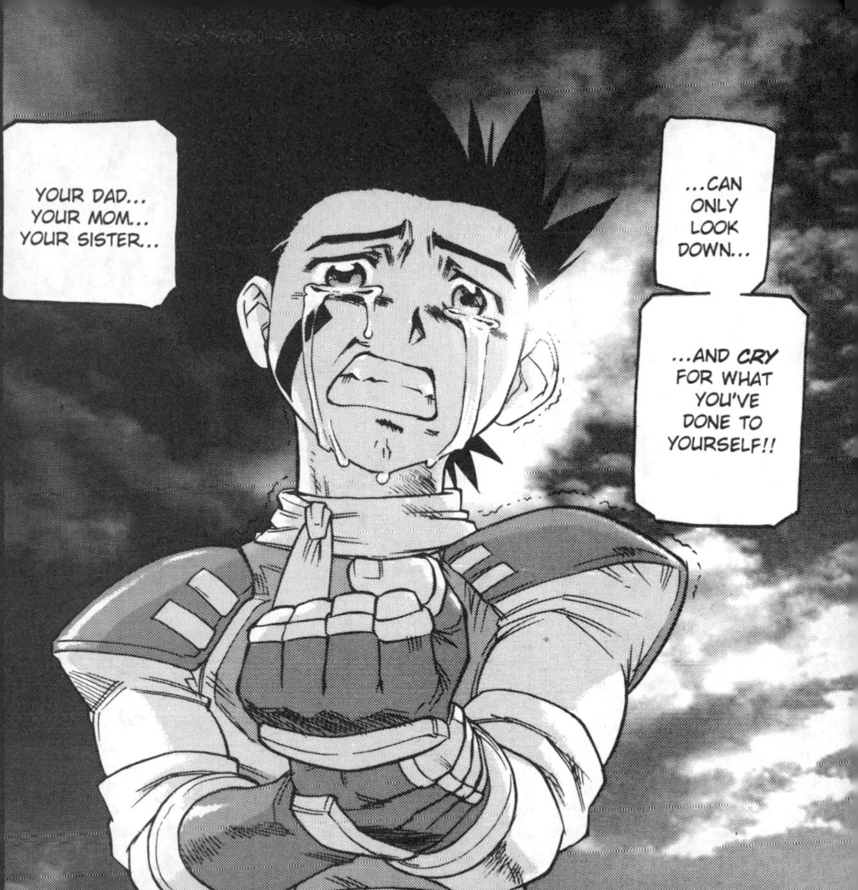
YOUR DAD... YOUR MOM... YOUR SISTER...
...CAN ONLY LOOK DOWN...
...AND CRY FOR WHAT YOU'VE DONE TO YOURSELF!!
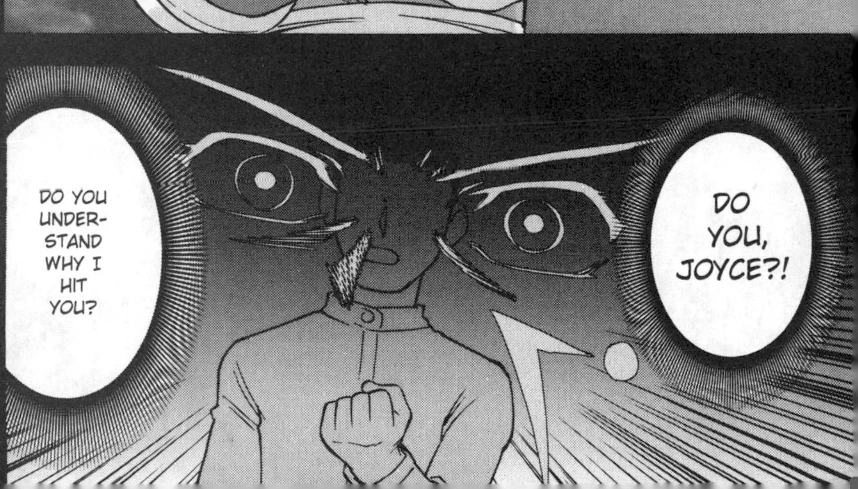
DO YOU UNDER-STAND WHY I HIT YOU?
DO YOU, JOYCE?!

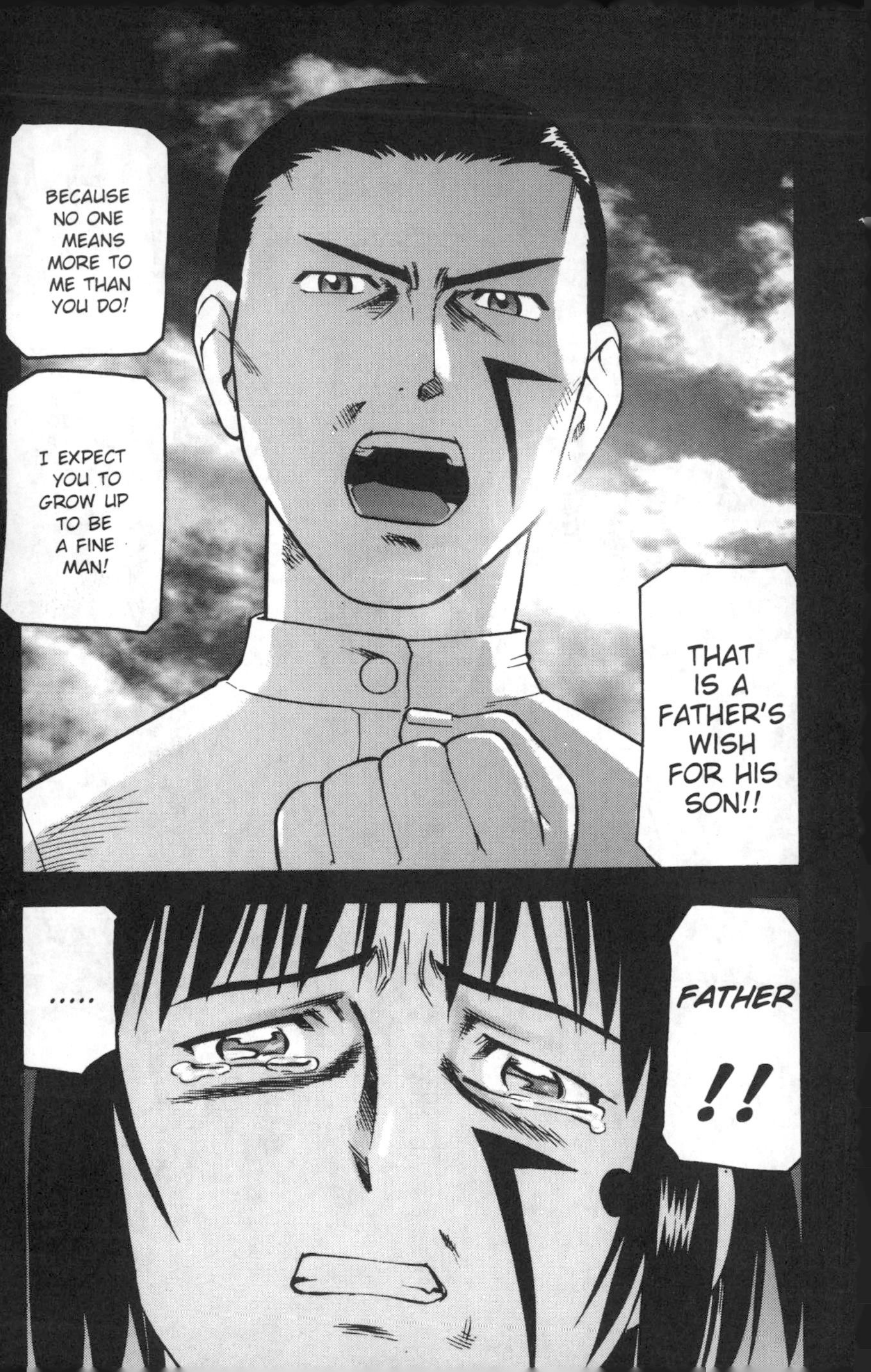
BECAUSE NO ONE MEANS MORE TO ME THAN YOU DO!
I EXPECT YOU TO GROW UP TO BE A FINE MAN!
THAT IS A FATHER'S WISH FOR HIS SON!!
.....
FATHER !!

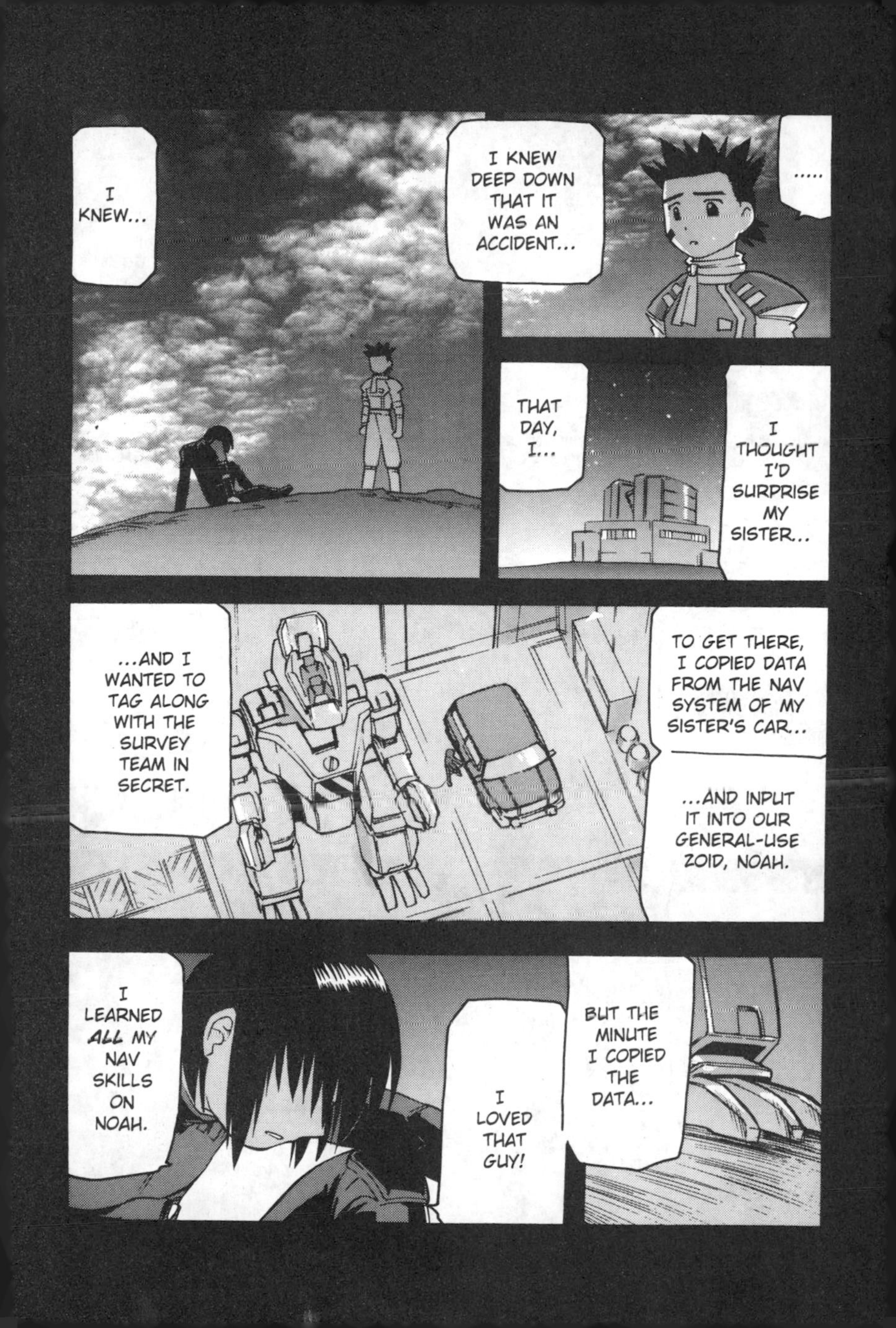
I KNEW...
I KNEW DEEP DOWN THAT IT WAS AN ACCIDENT...
.....
THAT DAY, I...
I THOUGHT I'D SURPRISE MY SISTER...
...AND I WANTED TO TAG ALONG WITH THE SURVEY TEAM IN SECRET.
TO GET THERE, I COPIED DATA FROM THE NAV SYSTEM OF MY SISTER'S CAR...
...AND INPUT IT INTO OUR GENERAL-USE ZOID, NOAH.
I LEARNED ALL MY NAV SKILLS ON NOAH.
I LOVED THAT GUY!
BUT THE MINUTE I COPIED THE DATA...

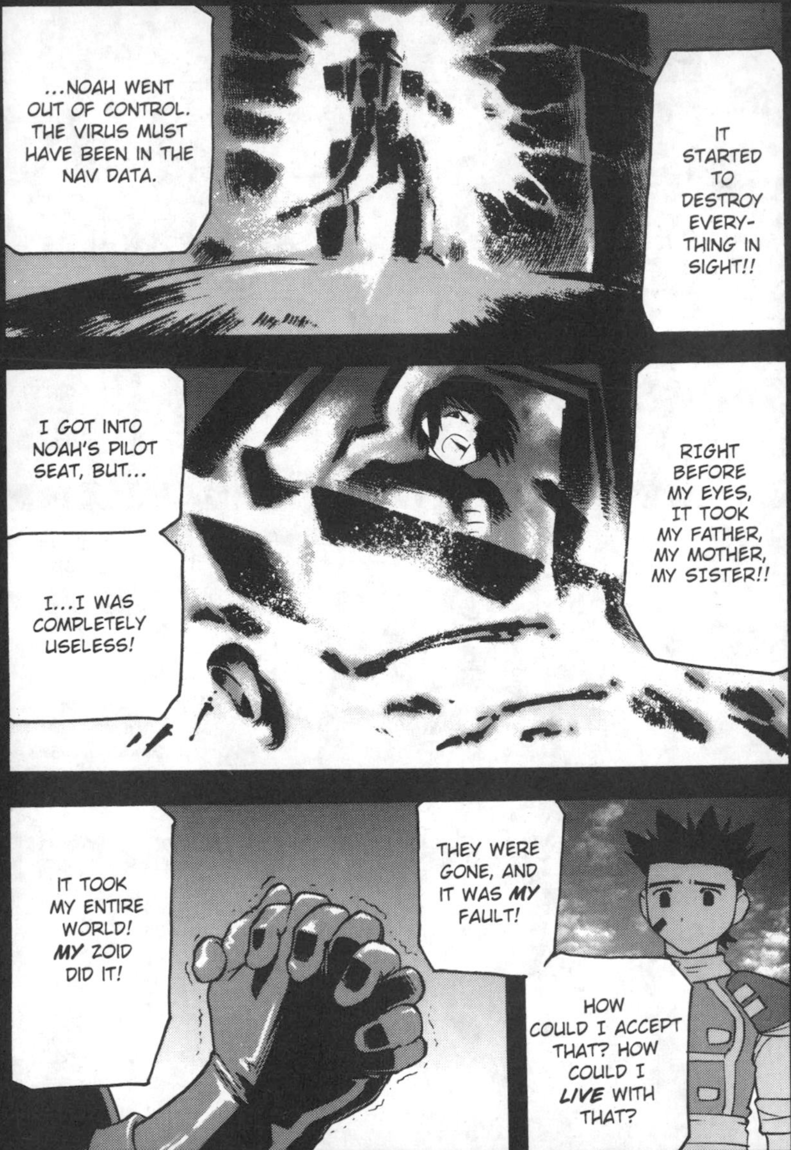
...NOAH WENT OUT OF CONTROL. THE VIRUS MUST HAVE BEEN IN THE NAV DATA.
IT STARTED TO DESTROY EVERY-THING IN SIGHT!!
I GOT INTO NOAH'S PILOT SEAT, BUT...
I...I WAS COMPLETELY USELESS!
RIGHT BEFORE MY EYES, IT TOOK MY FATHER, MY MOTHER, MY SISTER!!
IT TOOK MY ENTIRE WORLD! MY ZOID DID IT!
THEY WERE GONE, AND IT WAS MY FAULT!
HOW COULD I ACCEPT THAT? HOW COULD I LIVE WITH THAT?

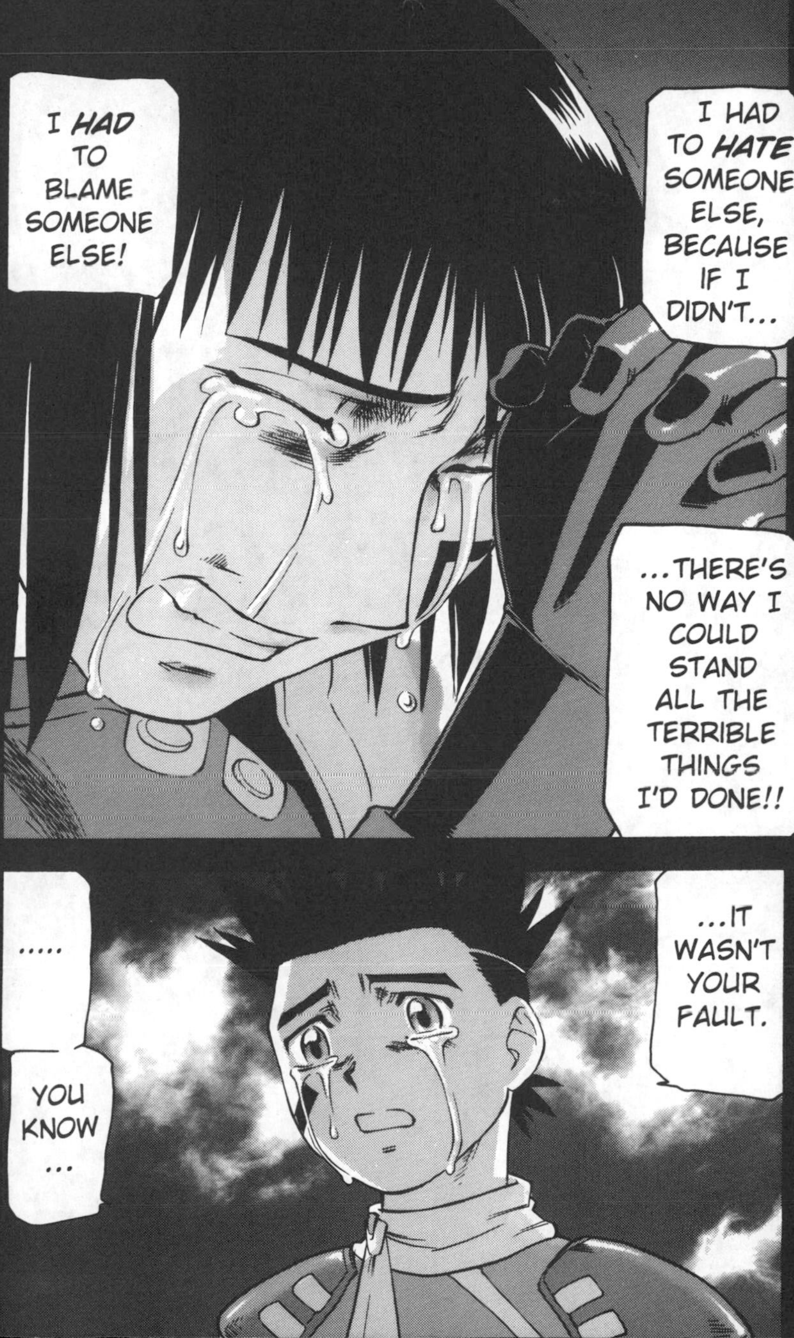
I HAD TO BLAME SOMEONE ELSE!
I HAD TO HATE SOMEONE ELSE, BECAUSE IF I DIDN'T...
...THERE'S NO WAY I COULD STAND ALL THE TERRIBLE THINGS I'D DONE!!
.....
YOU KNOW ...
...IT WASN'T YOUR FAULT.

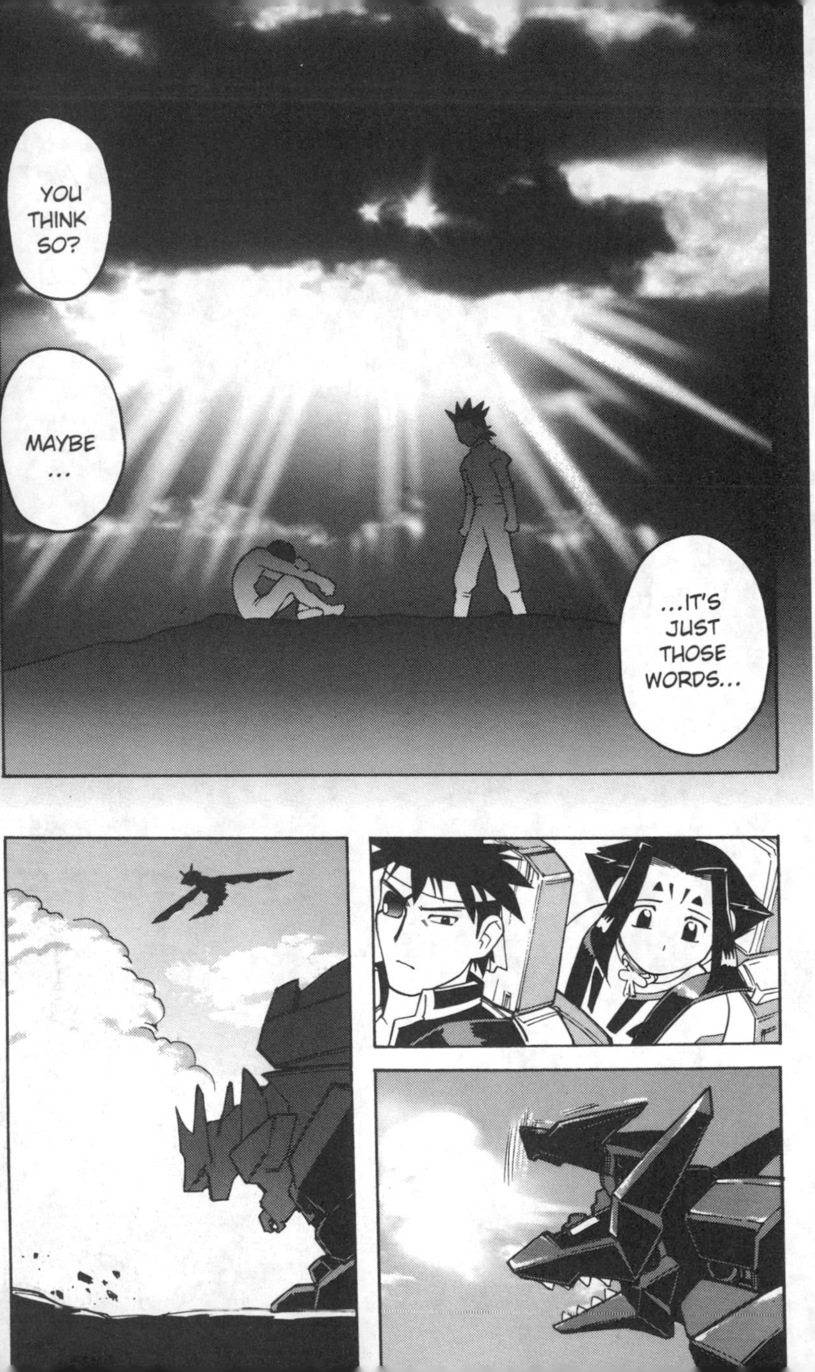
YOU THINK SO?
MAYBE ...
...IT'S JUST THOSE WORDS...

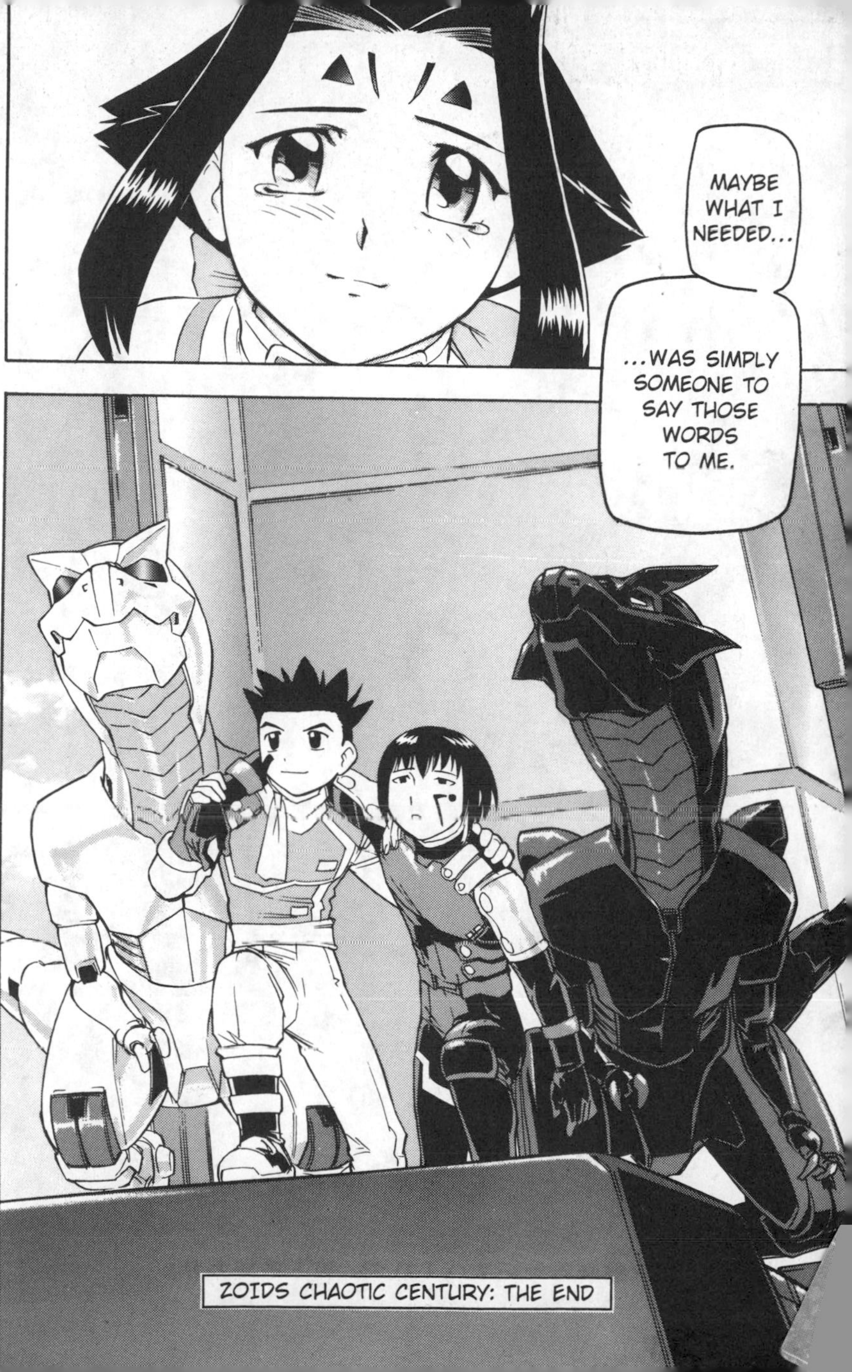
MAYBE WHAT I NEEDED...
...WAS SIMPLY SOMEONE TO SAY THOSE WORDS TO ME.
ZOIDS CHAOTIC CENTURY: THE END

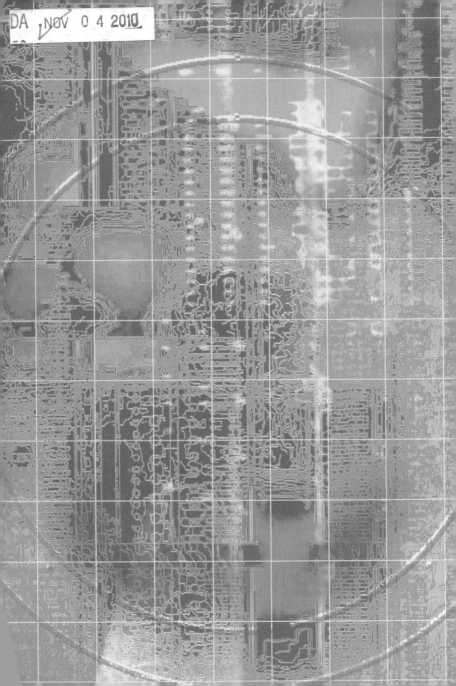